GOD

BELIEVES

IN

LOVE

GOD
BELIEVES
IN
LOVE

Straight Talk About Gay Marriage

GENE ROBINSON

ALFRED A. KNOPF   NEW YORK 2012

THIS IS A BORZOI BOOK PUBLISHED BY ALFRED A. KNOPF

Copyright © 2012 Gene Robinson
All rights reserved.
Published in the United States by Alfred A. Knopf,
a division of Random House, Inc., New York,
and in Canada by Random House of Canada Limited, Toronto.
www.aaknopf.com

Knopf, Borzoi Books, and the colophon are
registered trademarks of Random House, Inc.

Library of Congress Cataloging-in-Publication Data
Robinson, V. Gene, [date]
God believes in love : straight talk about gay marriage /
Gene Robinson. — 1st ed.
      p.   cm.
ISBN 978-0-307-95788-7
1. Same-sex marriage—Religious aspects—Episcopal Church.
2. Homosexuality—Religious aspects—Episcopal Church.
3. Marriage—Religious aspects—Episcopal Church.
4. Episcopal Church—Doctrines. I. Title.
BX5979.5.H65R63 2012
241'.63—dc23   2012023925

Jacket design by Oliver Munday

Manufactured in the United States of America

First Edition

DEDICATED TO
IMOGENE AND VICTOR ROBINSON, MY PARENTS,
AND THEIR INSPIRING SIXTY-FIVE-YEAR
MARRIAGE

CONTENTS

ACKNOWLEDGMENTS

There are so many people who deserve credit and thanks for helping me on this journey—both in my thinking and with the publication of this book.

To John Fortunato, whose writing unlocked the key to my closet door more than twenty-five years ago. To the leadership of Freedom to Marry's Evan Wolfson, who saw and understood the importance of marriage long before most of us, and kept singing his beautiful song to our community until we understood. To all the pioneers of our movement on whose shoulders I am privileged to stand.

To my book agent, Doug Abrams, who called me out of the blue and suggested that I might have this book in me—and then stuck around to shepherd me through the entire process with patience, encouragement, and a genuine commitment to this issue. Remarkable for a straight guy! I expected only an agent, but got a friend.

To my editor at Knopf, Vicky Wilson, whose critical eye and tough questions helped me at every turn. This book would not have happened without her brilliant and professional savvy.

To those gay or lesbian couples who have paved the way for all by sailing the largely uncharted waters of gay relationships: Dan and Russ, Tim and James, Mary and Nancy, Bruce and Barry, Jim and Paul, Mary and Sue, Macky and Nick, Steve and Don, Thad and George. You know who you are—and I hope you know how much you have inspired and taught me.

To the two most wonderful daughters a man could ever hope for, Jamee and Ella, for their love and devotion, and for the patience they have shown in loving me no matter what. And for our granddaughters, Morgan and Megan, who may well grow up in a world where having two dads (or granddads) or two moms may be no big deal.

Finally, to the two people who have taught me the most about marriage by being in a marriage with me: my former wife, "Boo" Martin, and my husband, Mark Andrew. For thirteen years, in our younger days, Boo and I forged a relationship that, in the end, still endures after our divorce. And for the last twenty-five years, Mark has stood by me as my friend, cheerleader, and most fervent supporter. In 2010, when marriage equality came to New Hampshire, I added one more important and cherished name for him: husband. There are simply no words to describe how indebted I am to him.

GOD

BELIEVES

IN

LOVE

INTRODUCTION

I believe in marriage.

Sixty-five years ago, Victor Robinson married his high school sweetheart, Imogene Bowman, both of them at the tender age of twenty. If there ever was a marriage made in heaven, this was it. Some fifteen months later, they welcomed their firstborn into the world. I was a very mixed blessing, given that I was massively injured in childbirth and not expected to live. Being very young and very poor, my parents were ill equipped to handle a newborn whose prognosis for ever walking or talking was not good. But they dealt with this seeming tragedy with the same love and devotion that characterized their marriage.

Victor and Imogene lived in rural Kentucky as tobacco sharecroppers. They worked twelve hours a day, except for Sunday, which was the Lord's day. My parents were descended from the founding members of Bethany Christian Church, a small congregation of the Disciples of Christ denomination. Living without running water or indoor plumbing, and with our community as our only support, my family loved the church, and it was our primary social outlet. I was steeped in and nourished by a constant study of Scripture, leading to my taking Jesus as my personal Lord and Savior, and my baptism with full immersion, at age twelve. My greatest desire was to lead a Christ-centered life.

At the same time, there was a growing self-understanding that I was different—and not in a positive way. There was no good name for what I was feeling. Homosexuality was almost never spoken of, and when it was, it was always in hushed tones, as if even saying the word made the notion more real and more acceptable than it deserved to be. More often, I would hear only of people who were "that way." Long before a world that would contain the likes of *Will & Grace, Ellen,* or an openly gay Billie Jean King, there were no role models of healthy, happy gay or lesbian people. Bisexual or transgender people were unimaginable. Allen Ginsberg, Malcolm Boyd, and other gay pioneers may have existed, but they were completely unknown to a farm kid in Kentucky.

In my early teens, friends of mine somehow obtained a copy of a *Playboy* magazine. As we were all looking at it, I became aware that these pictures (hardly revealing at all, compared with today's standards) were doing more for my friends than for me. And almost instantly, I perceived that to admit that these pictures were not stimulating to me would put my friendships—and possibly my physical safety—in jeopardy. I knew there was only one thing I could do. I pretended to be someone I was not.

Increasingly, I began to worry that I was more attracted to boys than to girls. I knew well from my religious upbringing that such a reality was repugnant to God. People like that were an "abomination" to God, and being deeply religious myself, and loving God "with all my heart, soul, mind, and strength," I found this an almost unbearable possibility. I prayed unceasingly for it not to be true, and if it were true, for God to change me. But that prayer was not answered.

The month I graduated from college, the Stonewall riot—the symbolic launch of the gay rights movement—occurred in New York City, but of course I knew nothing about that event. By the time I discerned my call to ordination and headed off to seminary, I was pretty sure that I was attracted to men. "Gay" was not yet a word generally used to describe homosexuals, but I knew what I was, and I didn't like it. Hardly a minute went by that I didn't loathe myself.

I set about the task of getting myself "cured." I liked women and had always had great relationships with my female friends. Surely, with enough help—from God and a good therapist—I could live my dream: to meet and fall in love with a young woman, get married, and have a family. Therapy twice a week for two years resulted in my feeling ready for such a relationship, and during a stint as a chaplain intern at the University of Vermont, I did meet a wonderful young woman. Within two weeks of meeting her, I confessed that virtually all of my relationships (very few, to be honest) had been with men but that through therapy I had changed. I believed with all my heart that I had changed. But about a month before the wedding, I broke down in tears one night, wondering aloud to my wife-to-be if this attraction to men might one day "rear its ugly head." She comforted me and said, "If that happens, we love each other enough to deal with it." A year after meeting, we were indeed married.

Being married was a dream come true for me, meeting and finding someone I wanted to share my life with, the prospect of having a soul mate and a family. It brought not only the sense of completion in my life but also a long-desired feeling of being "normal." Finally, after years of pain, I felt a part of the mainstream. I was now partnered with someone with whom I shared personal and public values, who had an entrepreneurial spirit similar to mine, and who wanted children as much as I did.

Not only did I love my wife, but I loved being married. What an extraordinary experience and privilege it was. I had stumbled upon someone I admired, respected, and loved. I was swept up in the heavenly knowledge that I was now bound together with someone who not only loved me as much as I loved her but was just as committed as I was to living out the rest of our lives together, through good times and bad. Difficult and painful times brought with them the opportunity to know her better, more deeply, more intimately. We shared moments of despair, when our dreams of founding a retreat center seemed to be dashed on the rocks of financial reality. We struggled to initiate two businesses simultaneously, knowing that failure would threaten our very survival. We worked side by side, eighteen hours a day, to create a new life together. The joyful and celebratory times made me feel as if I were the luckiest man on earth. The births of our two daughters added a whole new, almost sublime, dimension to our relationship, and we tried to become good parents. The love we felt for our daughters deepened our own love and commitment to each other. It seemed to many people—and often to ourselves—that we were the perfect couple.

But there was also something else going on deep within me. During that time, despite every effort on my part to suppress my feelings and emotions, I could not resist the reality beginning to invade my perfect life that I was drawn toward people of the same gender. As much as I loved my wife, as committed as I was to the nurturing of our children, as much as I valued our common life, I knew I was not whole and was not being truthful to myself, to my wife, or to God. In time, I came to understand that "gay" was who I was, not just what I was drawn to do. I had countless late-night talks with my wife and frequent visits to my therapist. My marriage was so important to me, so intrinsic to who I was, we tried hard together to make it work. After all, we had promised each other "until death do us part."

I began to make peace not only with myself but with God. I studied and restudied the Scriptures to see if the traditional understanding of those verses that condemned homosexuality really meant what I had been taught they meant. As a faithful Christian and a priest of the Church, I could not and would not merely brush Scripture aside, but rather I had to go deeper. In the end, I came to believe that being gay was no better and no worse than being straight and that like everyone else I was a child of God, loved by God beyond my wildest imagining. The problem was not with God loving me. The problem was with loving myself.

Ours had been the perfect marriage, or so the world thought. We jointly ran a girls' horseback-riding summer camp, and ours was the kind of relationship those girls hoped for in their own futures. They saw us interacting with each other in a loving and mutually supportive way. They admired our ability to work shoulder to shoulder together 24/7 and marveled at how we not only worked for our own success but also reached out to the world. They would often tell us how inspired they were by our example.

On the Sunday we knew we were going to tell our daughters, then eight and four years old, that we were getting a divorce, I was preaching at a local church, and my wife and young daughters were ushering. No fewer than twenty people commented that morning about how we were the perfect family. We knew otherwise, and over the previous couple of years we had come to understand that *both* of us were paying too high a price for being in this relationship.

We took our wedding vows seriously. As religious, faithful people, we did not take lightly the fact that we had said those vows in church, before God, and that we had invited God into our marriage. In an odd way, we believed that God was leading us to make the decision to separate and divorce. If we were going to end our relationship, we wanted to do so honorably and lovingly.

In the Episcopal wedding service, at the exchange of rings, the bride and the groom say, "I give you this ring as a symbol of my vows, and with all that I am, and all that I have, I honor you in the Name of God." Our joint and separate therapy, our prayers, and our endless, soul-searching conversations led us to believe that the only way to keep that vow—to honor each other in the Name of God—was to let each other go. That realization broke our hearts. In every other way, we were a deliriously happy couple, and our marriage had been the source of deep joy and happiness. How could we sacrifice all that, split up our family, subject our children to divorce, disappoint our friends and families, and start new, separate lives, all over the issue of sexuality? It seemed like a reckless thing to do, and yet we saw no other way to live a life of integrity. How could making such a decision seem so right and yet be so painful, all at the same time?

We brought a priest with us to the judge's chambers for the final divorce hearing. The meeting with the judge appeared amicable enough. After all, we still loved each other deeply! I felt as if I were cutting off my own arm or leg, a part of me that shaped who I was. Wasn't I crazy to be doing this? We had more love, more happiness, than anyone we knew. Why would we mess this up?! And yet whispering in my other ear was a voice—the still, small voice of God?—"be true to yourself," "live your life with as much integrity as you can muster," "trust Me that this is the path I'm calling you toward." It was excruciating.

After the divorce hearing, we followed the priest back to his parish and ended our marriage just as it had begun: in church. There was no liturgy for the ending of a marriage, so far as we knew. So we made it up out of whole cloth, in the context of the Communion service. I felt sadder than I had ever felt in my life. So sad I could hardly breathe. At the time of the confession, I remember saying over and over again, "I am so, so sorry." Indeed, each of us asked the other's forgiveness for all that had happened. The prayers we prayed were for each other, for healing from all this pain, and for our futures apart. And then, in the worst moment of all, heart-stoppingly painful, we prayed for our daughters—hoping against hope that we would not harm them too much in what we were about to do. With every ounce of commitment we could muster, we pledged our-selves to the joint raising and nurturing of our children. And then, in one of the holiest, most healing moments of my life, we gave our wedding rings back to each other as the symbol of our wedding vows that we no longer held each other to. And then we shared the Body and Blood of Christ in a service of Holy Communion. I don't know if there was ever a time, before or since, when I was in such need of God's sustenance. I don't know how we did it, to be honest. It felt as exquisitely holy as it was excruciatingly painful. Somehow we had managed to end our marriage in a loving way and not just slink away from God under cloak of night.

The experience of being married and then divorced did not make me doubt the institution or practice of marriage. Instead, I believed in marriage even more deeply. I was more convinced than ever that, as the Episcopal prayer book says in the marriage service, marriage "signifies to us the mystery of the union between Christ and his Church, and Holy Scripture commends it to be honored among all people." The question, of course, for this newly openly gay man, was whether the gift of marriage was also meant for same-gender couples—maybe even for me. Even twenty-five years ago, although I could scarcely articulate it, I believed the answer was yes.

A year and a half later, and two months after my former wife had remarried, I walked onto a beach in St. Croix and met Mark Andrew. I was instantly attracted to him, and I felt like a sixteen-year-old with a mad crush on someone. I loved everything about him. I loved that he had spent his adult life working for the Peace Corps and had served two years as a Peace Corps volunteer in Côte d'Ivoire, returning to the States to recruit other volunteers. I loved that he was training for a marathon. (I had never been a runner, and I admired his discipline.) He seemed so even and stable, a counterpoint to my flights of spontaneous exuberance. He had a great mind, and we soon discovered that we were both political junkies. And he was so damned handsome!

For the next year and a half, we talked on the phone every

night and visited each other every other weekend. Finally, it became clear to us that our commitment to each other was to make a life and family together. I had told Mark, soon after meeting him, that if this relationship became serious, he should know that I had no intention of leaving my daughters. I expressed the seriousness with which I took my parenting, and I meant to be intimately involved in their lives. Our decision to "be together" meant his leaving his career and friends and moving to New Hampshire. Such a decision is one that (mostly) brides have made for centuries to be with their husbands, but it felt very new for a man to be making such a sacrifice for another man.

My daughters at first, I think, loved the fact that their dad was happier than they had seen him in years. And then they began to love Mark too, for himself. They loved hearing his stories from the Peace Corps—especially his descriptions of eating exotic (and sometimes disgusting) things. They began to understand that he would guide, correct, and nurture them. Over the years, they came to value him as another dad—one who could and would give them a more objective view than either of their biological parents.

And for the first time in my life, my heart and my body felt in harmony. For the first time, I was able to express my love for someone *through* my body. In a way I had never before experienced, I understood what the prayer book means when it describes marriage as a union "in heart, body, and mind." I experienced a wholeness and integration between body and spirit I had only dreamed about. I remember thinking, "So *this* is what all the fuss is about! No wonder people like—and hallow—this!"

The greatest test of our relationship presented itself when I began to feel called by God to be a bishop. Mark had not exactly signed on for that! While we did not fully understand the anger and vitriol that would be unleashed if I were elected bishop, we certainly knew it would be controversial and would throw us into the spotlight of public attention. Mark is a private person, and being in the limelight was the last thing he ever wanted. He not only was willing to walk with me down that dangerous path but did so with unwavering support. We did not at the time know how dangerous it would be and how far some people's fear and hatred could go. We didn't know that our life together would now contain multiple death threats (almost daily, in the beginning). We would never have anticipated that Mark would spend his time at my public appearances scanning the crowd for possible attackers and assassins. Sometimes it's better that you *don't* know what lies ahead. In the troublesome years that have followed my election, Mark has been my chief cheerleader, trusted partner, and safe harbor in the storm. Every day, without fail, I marvel at the power of love and thank God that such was our commitment to each other—all without benefit of marriage, from society or the Church.

That too was about to change. Mark and I had been together since 1987. And on June 7, 2008, twenty-one years after we fell in love, and thanks to the law passed by the legislature and signed by the governor of New Hampshire, Mark and I became legal partners in a civil union. Although we were not yet allowed to be legally married, I had a very specific reason for wanting to legalize our relationship at that moment.

I was about to go to the Lambeth Conference of bishops in England. Although the Archbishop of Canterbury had chosen not to invite me (the first such exclusion of a duly elected and consecrated bishop in the history of the conference, dating back to the mid-nineteenth century), I had decided to go and make a witness anyway. The death threats against me had reignited with the announcement of my intention to be present, at least peripherally, at the Lambeth Conference of bishops, and I worried about Mark and his future, if something should happen to me. Because New Hampshire had made civil unions legal, I wanted to provide Mark with the protections such a union would offer if something did happen to me.

On January 1, 2010, Mark became my legal husband in marriage. Astoundingly, marriage equality in the eyes of the State had become the law in New Hampshire, and on the first day of 2010 our civil union was "converted" into a legal marriage. When our certificate of marriage arrived some weeks later in the mail, I held it in my hands, trembling with joy and in sheer disbelief and thinking, "Can this really be? Could this actually be happening to me, in my lifetime?" Such a possibility would never have entered my mind growing up. If something is simply and absolutely impossible, you don't even dream of it. And yet here it was.

What I can tell you is that everything I intended and pledged in my marriage to a woman I intended and pledged in my marriage to a man. It feels like the same thing, being lived out with the one I love. It has the same trials and tribulations, the same joys and rewards. Marriage calls us to be our best selves, for each other. Marriage is the very human attempt to make a place in one's heart for another—a place so holy as to make it possible to have a love for another at times greater than the love of one's self.

And that is why, for the Church, marriage is a sacrament. A sacrament is one of the places God promises to show up! It is in learning to love another as much as or more than one loves one's self that we get a tiny glimpse of the selfless love that God has for each of us. It is in marriage that we have the opportunity to experience and learn about God's unconditional love for us.

Nothing in Scripture or orthodox theology precludes our opening the institution of marriage to same-gender couples. Those who oppose marriage equality for gay or lesbian couples, pleading for us not to "redefine" marriage, do not understand that gay marriage only builds up the traditional meaning of marriage. We are *not* changing its meaning but merely revising the list of those to whom it is available. Not unlike the rather recent opening of legal marriage to interracial couples, the legal marriage of two same-gender people retains the traditional meaning of marriage while expanding the number of people whom it may benefit.

This book is a conversation between myself and the reader, a conversation that tries to answer all the major questions I have heard over and over again from good and loving people who are trying to understand whether gay marriage is truly a just and righteous path for our states, for our country, and for our world.

By now, most Americans know someone who is gay—perhaps a son or daughter, a nephew or niece, a co-worker, a former classmate. And now, because they love this gay person and know of his or her desire or intention to be married to someone of the same gender, they have to ask the "marriage question" in a new way, in order to maintain their relationship with that beloved son or daughter, niece or nephew or co-worker. Maybe the reader is a parent (or an aunt or uncle, or grandmother) asked to be present for a gay or lesbian child's wedding and is feeling uncomfortable with the whole thing. Perhaps the reader's hairstylist or dentist or church organist is getting married to his or her same-gender partner and wonders whether it's a good idea to attend. Or perhaps the reader is a member of a religious denomination that accepts gay marriage, but cannot understand how this can be what God wants. Perhaps the reader is a clergyperson struggling to reconcile his traditional religious teaching with his own experience of loving, faithfully partnered gay couples. Perhaps the reader is an employer and has trouble understanding why marital benefits should be extended to his married gay workers. Or perhaps the reader is simply someone who knows this to be one of the great issues of our time and wants to understand it from the viewpoint of those who are seeking to make such a change.

Each of the questions that is frequently posed to me, as an openly gay, married man and as a bishop of the Church, forms a chapter in this book.

This is a contentious issue, both for society in general and for religious people in particular. Citizens of goodwill in this and other countries, as well as thoughtful, prayerful people of faith, honestly disagree on this issue. Society and our religious communities claim to respect the dignity of every human being. The right and opportunity to marry the person one loves are essential to that respect and dignity. I hope you will walk a few steps with me. And together we might come to a place where the traditional meaning of marriage not only survives intact but is indeed deepened and renewed in its profound importance to the well-being of our society, even as we open this beloved institution to couples who have not yet been free to enjoy its many blessings.

CHAPTER I

Why Gay Marriage Now?

I was born in 1947. Homosexuality was hardly ever referred to in polite conversation, and even when it was, it was always in a whisper. "Gay" wasn't even a word yet used to mean "homosexual." Veiled references were either polite ("he's a bit 'that way,' isn't he?") or derogatory and stereotypical ("he's a bit 'light in the loafers,' don't you think?").

Homosexuality was something known to exist in certain exotic communities—mostly among actors and beat poets like Allen Ginsberg. No one in the hinterlands knew of the Mattachine Society for gay men and the Daughters of Bilitis for lesbians, secretive, emerging gay organizations in the 1950s on the liberal coasts. Certainly no one dreamed that romantic movie icons like Rock Hudson and James Dean, who were leading men wooing Hollywood's most beautiful women, were homosexual.

Those in my generation could go through their entire lives without ever being asked the question, "Are you straight or gay?" It simply wasn't on the radar screen for most Americans. Nor was it on mine.

It is hard to describe, then, the isolation I experienced as a boy when I started feeling "different." There was no language to put around it. I wouldn't have imagined that anyone else in the world was feeling what I was feeling. But I knew, from an early age, that I was different.

It didn't help when my uncle Buck started calling me a "sissy." I'm sure he wasn't thinking "homosexual," but he did seem to sense that I was different, not like his own son or other boys. "Effeminate," he might have said, if he had even known the word. Not like the masculine boy I was supposed to be. I hated him, and I feared him, because he seemed to know my little, horrifying secret, and he would communicate it to the world at our family gatherings, with all the cruelty he could muster.

The only place homosexuality was discussed, albeit in a veiled and cryptic way, was at church. From time to time, there would be diatribes about "a man lying with a man" being an abomination. While I had never, ever gone as far as imagining lying with another man, somehow I took these sermons personally. I didn't need any more fear and isolation in my life. But these sermons, for reasons I couldn't explain, added the fear that I might be an "abomination" to the God of all creation.

Getting beaten up in the backyard at a classmate's house

party didn't help. It was nothing truly dangerous, but I did not defend myself when "friends" began to rough me up. It must be true, I thought. I really am a sissy. Not a man. And to this day I can remember the shame I felt at my father's obvious disappointment that I had not stood up for myself.

Thirty, even twenty years ago, most Americans would have told you that they didn't know anyone gay. They might have wondered, and even joked, about their weird uncle Harold, who acted a bit strange, even effeminate. And they might have mentioned, usually with good humor and genuine affection, those two ladies who have lived at the end of the street forever—you know, the ones who keep their lawn so nice?! But most Americans would have been telling the truth about not personally knowing anyone who acknowledged his or her same-gender attraction, not to mention doing so with pride and dignity.

While the riot at the Stonewall Inn in New York officially galvanized the modern gay rights movement, and people began to understand more fully that there were homosexuals in the world, it was the AIDS crisis of the 1980s that alerted people to the presence in their midst of men who had sex with men. It was in 1982 that *The New York Times* reported on a new phenomenon: growing numbers of men were dying of diseases previously almost unheard of. These opportunistic infections, normally kept at bay by a healthy immune system, were ravaging these previously healthy men. And these afflicted men were homosexuals. The word "gay" had come into the lexicon by this time, and it was used to describe these medical anomalies: gay cancer.

As men started to get sick, very sick, they began calling home from San Francisco, West Hollywood, and New York. They were calling their parents and brothers and sisters to say that they were dying. Yes, I have the "gay cancer." Yes, I'm gay—and my "friend," whom you have come to enjoy and love over the years, is my lover. And yes, he's taking care of me. Except that he's getting sick too. And dying, like me.

Men from little towns and hamlets all over America who had lived the "gay life" in secret, in faraway places, were calling home to say, "I'm sick with the gay disease." And in countless homes all across America, mothers and fathers and siblings knew for the first time—or had their suspicions confirmed—that their son or brother was gay.

Lesbians were increasingly outed by the same experience. Having also moved to places of acceptance and affirmation in large cities, they had come to know their gay brothers who were now becoming sick. Many of them took care of their seriously ill gay friends. Many began to advocate for AIDS funding and treatment. Many sat with their gay friends and listened to the devastating fallout from coming-out to their parents. Many shared the pain of coming clean about who they were and whom they loved. And as a result, many of them felt called to come out to their own parents as lesbian—partly in solidarity with their gay brothers, and partly because they too wanted to live free from keeping secrets from the families they loved.

Increasingly, even those not infected with the virus that came to be known as HIV wanted this same freedom. Despite the terrible consequences of coming out experienced by many, there were enough success stories to make them wonder, "What if I came out to *my* parents? Would they still love me?" And so, in ever larger numbers, the calls or visits home began, for the purpose of coming out.

In countless living rooms across America, beloved sons and daughters sat down, hearts in their throats, to say, "Mom, Dad. I'm gay." It is hard to describe the cataclysmic, earthquake-like effect this had on families. Something simply unthinkable had been revealed, although to be honest, many parents had wondered why their son or daughter hadn't married, or didn't even seem to be dating, or simply had become silent about his or her personal life. Now it all made sense—terrible and horrifying sense. Those whose sons were now sick with AIDS had a double whammy: they hardly knew which to grieve first, the revelation that they had a gay son or the fact that he was dying at age twenty-eight.

Remember how social change happens. Each of us has a worldview that pretty much interprets the world for us, puts our personal and public experiences in some kind of rational and understandable order. That worldview works fairly well for a period of time. Then something happens that renders it insufficient. Something happens that can't be fit into life as we have known and interpreted it. Something so shocking and disturbing as to shake the very foundations of who we thought we were.

Parents across America knew they loved their sons. They were proud of them and bragged to relatives and friends about what they were accomplishing, albeit far away in San Francisco. They had learned not to ask too many personal questions, and there was often a feeling of something unspoken. But still, what a wonderful son he was!

And now this! Was he going to stay where he was, nursed by his "partner"? (What a strange new meaning to the word!) How could a parent explain to the neighbors these now-frequent trips to San Francisco, which clearly went beyond the annual visit? Or was he going to come home to die, to be cared for by his parents? And how could that be explained to nosy relatives—especially when they saw how emaciated he looked, with the telltale, dark reddish splotches of Kaposi's Sarcoma beginning to appear on his face? The son's coming-out to his parents often involved the parents' coming-out to their family and friends—not a willing, voluntary coming-out as having a gay son, but one born of necessity and tragedy.

And so the parents were having an experience for which their comfortable worldview had not prepared them. They knew two things for sure: their son was gay, and they loved him. More often than not, this felt like being placed between a rock and a hard place. Being gay (what a strange word for a condition so tragic and so morally disgusting) was a terrible thing. But this was their son, whom they had always loved. And the family was thrown into emotional chaos, a battle between two competing truths. Over time, each family resolved this issue. For the unlucky ones, the gay son was disowned, pushed away, and condemned out of moral outrage and (usually) religious rigidity. For the lucky ones, the urge to love overcame the need to judge, and with tentative and uncertain steps these parents began to change their long-held worldview, to allow for the possibility that their child's homosexuality might not be the end of the world, nor would it precipitate the end of their love for him.

In biblical imagery, the scales had fallen from their eyes. What was previously unknown or only suspected was confirmed. Now they knew. And so would everyone else. Parents would often experience an isolation of their own, fearing to tell friends and family the truth, lest they be blamed for their son's homosexuality. After all, wasn't it something they had done, or not done, that had made him this way? What would people think of them?

Simultaneous with the emergence of AIDS, and largely because of it, gay organizations took on a new courage and boldness. Groups like Act Up loudly proclaimed the presence of gay people: "We're here. We're queer. Get used to it!" Those who resisted a vigorous response to the HIV/AIDS crisis, including gay men and lesbians who were unaffected by the pandemic, were challenged by "Silence =

Death." Harvey Milk, the first openly gay politician to be elected to public office in the previous decade, had said, "Coming-out is the most political thing you can do." It turned out he was right. And as more and more gay men and lesbians came out to their families and friends— not because they had to, but because they wanted to— Americans realized that they knew someone gay or lesbian. And our world irrevocably changed.

In the years to come, other sexual minorities would be inspired to follow the lead of their gay brothers and lesbian sisters. People who were open to physical intimacy with people of either gender would come out as bisexual. And then we began to hear from people whose physical characteristics and genitals indicated one gender but whose feelings and inner being indicated the opposite. Transgender people are still in the early stages of coming-out, but because their very existence challenges our comfortable definitions of gender identity and expression (even for gay men and lesbians), it has been a difficult journey forward. The murder rate for open and honest transgender people is horrifyingly high. It is still a dangerous world for those who have come to know and acknowledge themselves as transgender. Transgender and bisexual people have joined their gay brothers and lesbian sisters in confronting their families with the truth about their lives.

High school and college reunions have often provided an opportunity for learning about people (not to mention humor!). It is very common for someone to show up at his or her reunion not with a spouse of the opposite gender but with a same-gender partner. This can come as a shock to a former classmate who only remembers you as the good-looking, girl-chasing captain of the football team. For some, it's simply not on their radar screen. When Mark and I attended his reunion at Middlebury College and I was introduced to a friend as his "partner," the clueless friend asked what *business* we were in.

Even more dramatic is the reunion where good ol' Jack arrives back at his alma mater as Jacqueline, now a woman and looking pretty damn good! As the stigma against transgender people diminishes and more transgender people find the world safe enough to tell their stories, we will see more of this.

As much as some would like all this to have never occurred, or for the world to go back to a "simpler" time when "men were men, and women were women, and everyone knew the difference," the fact is that toothpaste is never going back into the tube. This is a new reality, and like it or not, the world has to deal with it.

With this newly acknowledged existence of lesbian, gay, bisexual, and transgender people in our midst—members of our families, next-door neighbors, former classmates, colleagues in the workplace, not to mention on TV and in the culture—a new awareness of the needs and aspirations of this group is emerging. With it, there is a growing understanding that this group has been discriminated against, not merely in a personal, individual way, but also in a societal structure that systematically rewards hetero-sexuals and punishes homosexuals, just as whites have been rewarded at the expense of blacks and men rewarded at the expense of women. Beyond the personal issue of whether kind and compassionate treatment will be accorded gay individuals, this systemic discrimination embedded in our societal norms, laws, and rights is a justice issue that begs for redress.

Increasingly, lesbian, gay, bisexual, and transgender people are demanding that they be treated with the same dignity and afforded the same responsibilities and rights as their heterosexual fellow citizens. Public policies are begin-ning to change. We've seen the end of "Don't Ask, Don't Tell" in the military, and the White House has announced that it will no longer defend in court the so-called Defense of Marriage Act (DOMA), believing it to be unconstitu-tional. There is even increased opposition to DOMA in Congress. Such systemic discrimination now seems anti-quated and unfair to many. Challenges to state constitu-tional amendments barring gay marriage (and in some states, even the outlawing of civil unions and domestic part-nerships between people of the same gender) are under way. While there is still opposition to changing these policies, it is now a foregone conclusion that these policies are worthy of a vigorous debate and that lesbian, gay, bisexual, and transgender people may indeed have a legitimate and equal claim on the rights and privileges of citizenship in America.

In this context, the demand for marriage equality is not

surprising. After all, marriage is the State's way of promoting stability within society. Married couples are rewarded for their mutual commitments with tax benefits, insurance coverage, inheritance laws, and a host of other financial benefits. We are now living in a time of disconnect for many gay and lesbian couples who are legally married in their state of residence but still denied federal rights (including Social Security benefits and protections) because of the Defense of Marriage Act at the federal level.

But this debate isn't just about financial advantage. It's also about respect. Mutually committed couples of the same gender are increasingly demanding the societal and social respect that accrues from marriage—not just in America, but in many countries around the world. The burden is gradually but dramatically shifting from those who are arguing for equal treatment under the law to those who are having to explain why this equal treatment should *not* be the case. Perhaps no other shift in public opinion and public policy has occurred in such a short period of time, historically speaking. And we find ourselves talking about gay marriage in a way that would have been unimaginable only a few years ago. It is a conversation that is both particular (about rights, privileges, responsibilities, and benefits) and symbolic (about equal respect from the law and equal justice under the law). It is a conversation whose time has come.

CHAPTER 2

Why Should You Care About
Gay Marriage If You're Straight?

We have our own homegrown saint and martyr here in New Hampshire. Jonathan Myrick Daniels was born in Keene in 1939, entered Harvard in 1961, and experienced a call from God to enter the process toward ordination, expecting to be ordained to the priesthood in The Episcopal Church in 1966. In March 1965, Jonathan heeded the call by Dr. Martin Luther King Jr. for whites to come to Selma, Alabama, and join in a march to the capital of Montgomery. After the march, and feeling somewhat uncomfortable with merely breezing in for a weekend of protest, he decided to stay in Alabama and continue through the summer his advocacy for African-Americans.

On August 13, 1965, Jonathan was arrested with twenty-eight other protesters in Fort Deposit, Alabama, and was transported to and jailed in nearby Hayneville. Upon release, he and another priest, along with two African-American youths, were standing outside Varner's Grocery Store, where they went to buy a Coke. Tom L. Coleman, an engineer for the state highway department and an unpaid special deputy, came outside, threatening them with a shotgun. Coleman leveled his gun at seventeen-year-old Ruby Sales. Jonathan pushed her to the ground and took the full blast of Coleman's shotgun. He died instantly. The other priest was shot in the back as he escaped with the black youngsters. Coleman was exonerated by an all-white jury, but Jonathan's death seemed to help galvanize whites, especially white Episcopalians, all across America. In 1991, Jonathan Daniels was added to the list of saints with a special day of remembrance designated in the calendar of Lesser Feasts and Fasts for the Episcopal Church.

Beyond the obvious bravery and self-sacrifice of this twenty-six-year-old seminarian, what seems miraculous about Jonathan's witness is that here was a privileged northern white man who needn't have cared at all about an issue that did not necessarily affect him. He was living comfortably and headed toward a respected career, with his whole life ahead of him. What seems miraculous—and saintly—to me is that somehow he saw the struggle of southern African-Americans as his own struggle, took their suffering upon himself, and committed himself to their liberation as if their freedom and his own were inextricably linked.

The nineteenth-century American Jewish poet Emma Lazarus (yes, author of "Give me your tired, your poor, your huddled masses yearning to breathe free") got it right: "Until we are all free, we are none of us free."

For most straight people, the notion of two men or two women legally marrying each other would have never come into their minds if it hadn't been for the demands of gay men and lesbians for marriage equality. After all, the understanding of marriage as being between a man and a woman (or in earlier times, one man and as many women as he could afford!) had seemed settled for a very long time.

As a matter of fact, it was also "settled" for a very long time in the minds of gay and lesbian people. The judgment, prejudice, and even hatred toward anyone perceived to be homosexual were so harsh and so seemingly intractable there was hardly room to imagine legal marriage between two people of the same gender. It was virtually impossible to imagine a time when gay and lesbian (and later, bisexual and transgender) people would enjoy enough recognition and acceptance to have the luxury of contemplating the possibility of marriage equality.

In fact, in the early 1990s, there was a great debate in the gay community about whether marriage was something we should fight for. Most leaders of the gay community felt that other rights (for example, nondiscrimination in employment and public accommodation) were more achievable and more logical to pursue. In addition, those same leaders believed that "gay marriage" would be such a polarizing and explosive issue that the pursuit of it would result in a huge backlash against the entire gay community and deal a setback to achieving other civil rights for lesbian, gay, bisexual, and transgender people.

Only one national voice kept singing the song for marriage equality for gay and lesbian couples. Evan Wolfson, executive director of the then-quite-modest Freedom to Marry coalition, was the only person reciting, over and over, "Until we have marriage equality, we won't be equal. Anything less is second class." Despite the attempts of well-meaning people, both within and beyond the lesbian, gay, bisexual, and transgender community, to shut him up, or at least quiet him down, Evan kept at it. Over the years, he taught and inspired gay and lesbian people to dream of their own equality. Today, there is no state in the Union not dealing with marriage equality for gay and lesbian couples. Even if the efforts toward equality fail, still it is being debated only twenty years after it was unthinkable, thanks to Evan Wolfson and those who joined him in this movement.

If it was difficult to bring gay and lesbian couples themselves along in service to their own equality and liberation, then it is not surprising that many heterosexual people wonder why this should matter to *them*. After all, they have the right to marry. They have the right to divorce and remarry. To many heterosexuals, the whole notion of homosexuality is strange and a little creepy (and let's face it, the "creepy" part is the physical, sexual act), and the issue of marriage equality seems like a quest by a minority for more acceptance and legitimacy than they have a right to. Why would or should any heterosexual care?

Heterosexuals have good reason to consider the issues related to same-gender marriage because marriage equality is an issue "coming to a theater near you!" It won't be long before nearly everyone in America will be touched by this issue. Maybe you meet someone at work or at a dinner party who casually, or perhaps cautiously, reveals that he's gay. The new neighbors come over from next door to introduce themselves—and they're a lesbian couple. Someone in your family—a nephew or niece, brother or sister, uncle or cousin, even a son or daughter—not only reveals himself or herself to be gay but also wants you to meet the love of his or her life. And while you're still absorbing and adjusting to this news and trying not to show your discomfort, she announces that they have plans to marry and want you to come to the wedding. Believe me, this is happening or soon will—even if you're from a conservative state or part of a conservative religious community. And if it doesn't happen directly to you, it will happen to one of your friends who will come to you and ask, "What do you think? What should I do?" Sorting through what you think about same-gender marriage *now* is getting prepared for the inevitable.

The fact is, this discussion is occurring in every religion, every denomination, and virtually every nation on the planet. It is the civil rights issue of our time. Those religions and Christian denominations that are absolutely clear about their opposition to the legal marriage of two people of the same gender are having to deal with this issue no less than those in the liberal, progressive religions and denominations. After all, Orthodox Jews, conservative Muslims, and fundamentalist Christians are just as likely to raise a gay son or daughter as any other mother or father.

I once got an angry e-mail from a man in Texas who wanted to rail at me for my public pronouncements on this topic. As so often happens, he felt it necessary to rehearse for me his heterosexual credentials—a happy marriage, three beautiful children, a household of deep and conservative faith. He would never, he told me, allow any of his children to become gay. When I responded to his e-mail, I asked him, "What if you actually don't control whether one of your children comes to know themselves as gay or lesbian? Do you really want to have taken such a firm stand against homosexuality that you cut yourself off from a relationship with one of your children?" He wrote back, quite thoughtfully and vulnerably, that he had never quite considered such a possibility, given his conservative faith and his belief that his neat and tidy family would never find itself with a gay son or lesbian daughter. He was admitting, perhaps for the first time, that homosexuality and the desire to marry might touch him personally.

And so all people—whether parents, aunts, godparents, or next-door neighbors—need to consider what their reaction will be when a beloved son, daughter, niece, or godchild comes out and wants them to love the person he or she has fallen in love with.

Of course, there are much deeper and more significant reasons for dealing with the issue of homosexuality and the desire for marriage among same-gender couples, especially for people of faith. At its most basic, every religion known to humankind has some version of "do unto others as you would have them do unto you." Jesus did not originate the Golden Rule. Versions of it appear many centuries before Christ. It seems to be a part of the highest aspirations and moral makeup of humankind from the very beginning.

What would be the result of every person of faith, indeed every person with a desire to be a moral human being, thinking, "If that were me, what would I want?" This seems almost too simplistic to be serious. But I'm not sure it is an exercise engaged in by those adamantly opposed to gay marriage. "If I *were* gay . . ." is too big a stretch for those who find such a possibility so remote and so disgusting to even consider. There are those who almost casually say, "Well, if I were gay, I would understand that God doesn't hold that against me, as long as I don't act on it." That is a rather cavalier statement for a straight person to make on behalf of a gay man or lesbian. It is difficult to believe that any gay or lesbian person would be comfortable with or even resigned to that, much less happy.

The stories of gay and lesbian people over the last thirty years show that that is not the case. And let's remember, the part of this equation that says "God doesn't hold that against me" is a relatively new development. For countless centuries, it was *being* gay that was thought to be an abomination. For some people of faith, it still is. In their eyes and the eyes of the Creator they believe in, a homosexual person is damaged goods, something gone wrong in creation. Pulpits are full of preaching about "love the sinner, hate the sin," but to gay men and lesbians it still feels like "hate the person."

We still endure conservative Christian leaders who compare homosexuality to alcoholism—a sad, regrettable defect among a certain minority of us who have this characteristic of finding alcohol toxic to our systems. And the only answer to this tragic defect is complete abstinence from the drug of choice. It was not long ago that alcoholism was seen as a moral defect, a failure of will, and only recently that we have come to understand it is a medical condition. Only recently have we begun to move away from seeing the alcoholic as sinful and morally disdainful.

It is interesting to see conservative religious leaders and followers use this comparison. They have attempted to take "higher" ground and to sound both sympathetic and reasonable in asserting, "Well, there's nothing wrong with *being* gay, as long as you never indulge yourself in this horrific and God-condemned drug of choice." Initially, this sounds so much kinder and gentler than outright condemnation of being gay. But when analyzed more closely, it is hardly a step forward. Such "compassionate conservatism" has only been the reluctantly offered attitude when outright rejection of a beloved son or daughter or fellow church member has seemed too cruel. For countless centuries, outright rejection has been the order of the day.

What would a serious consideration of "do unto others as you would have them do unto you" look like? A quick, passing contemplation is not enough. Serious consideration would have one wondering what it would be like to grow up suspecting, even "knowing," that the God of all creation thinks I'm an "abomination." Imagine beginning the self-alienation at an early age: "There's something about me, integral to me, that I can never, ever share with anyone—and especially not those who love me, because it will certainly mean losing their love." Imagine pretending from adolescence onward that I am interested in and attracted to people I'm not interested in or attracted to— and at the same time stripping from my outward actions and words any indication of who I *am* interested in and attracted to. What does it do to a child to learn at a quite early age to filter absolutely everything I say—in the split second before I say it—to rid it of every indication of what is really going on with me? To learn as an adult to never mention to my co-workers what I did over the weekend and whom I did it with? To deflect all attempts by my well-meaning friends to set me up with someone of the opposite sex? To completely compartmentalize my life into the "respectable" parts versus the unspeakable parts? To feel "less than" in every possible way? And to live in constant fear that the real me will be discovered and everything I have worked for and hoped for will go down in shameful flames?

That is what it would mean to walk in a gay man's or lesbian's shoes—to sit with and contemplate what that kind of life would be. And then, of course, it gets worse. You imagine that given this hidden life, you meet someone and begin the tender, complicated, and exciting process of falling in love. You can't tell anyone—or just a few people who know about your secret. You can't share it with your parents, your siblings, your straight friends. You are happier than you've ever been in your whole life, and you have to keep it a secret. You are cut off from talking through this budding relationship with those who might help you answer the questions, "Am I really in love?" and "Is this the right person for me?" After all, we test out a new relationship by having a prospective partner meet our friends, seeing how she interacts with the people we know and love, and soliciting from our friends and family, "What did you think of her?" All of those normal ways of testing out a relationship are not open to you, unless you come out.

Given the burdens borne by gay and lesbian people, it's a wonder any of us survived to tell the tale. And I find it hard to believe that anyone who has seriously stopped long enough to contemplate such an existence would continue to want to deprive gay and lesbian people of the respect, companionship, and integrity we deserve. At its most basic, a religious commitment to "do unto others as you would have them do unto you" suggests that our views toward homosexuality and same-gender marriage have to change.

Still, as a straight person, you might say, "This just isn't my fight." No, it isn't. Unless you care about the kind of society we have. Unless you want the society of which you are a part to be a just one. Unless you believe that a free society, not to mention a godly religion, should fight injustice wherever it is found. Unless your religion tells you—as our entire Judeo-Christian heritage does—that any society will be judged by the way it treats its most vulnerable. Unless you care about our children. Unless fairness matters to you. Unless violence against lesbian, gay, bisexual, and transgender people concerns you. Unless "liberty and justice for all" is something you believe applies to all our citizens.

Deep within the Jewish, and therefore also Christian, heritage and history is a razor-sharp focus on heeding the cries for justice from those who are oppressed. Much of the Jewish Scriptures (called the "Old Testament" by Christians) are devoted to the stories of the prophets. Let's remember that in that tradition, a prophet is not one who foresees the future but rather one who is courageous enough to see the inequities, immoralities, and sins of the *present*. A prophet is the one who stands up and speaks truth to power. A prophet is one who risks his own neck to tell the powers that be what they least want to hear, who calls to account the behavior of the powerful and the wealthy, on behalf of the oppressed and the poor.

The prophet becomes the voice of the voiceless. Lest we trivialize this role, remember that the prophetic voice is not about mere whining but rather about speaking with moral and righteous authority about how God would have us act toward one another. The prophet is pleading not necessarily his own case but that of the oppressed and powerless minority who are being treated unjustly. Even the Psalms often articulate the cries for justice from the oppressed, calling upon God to ease their burdens, overturn their enemies, and restore justice to the world.

Jesus clearly understands himself to be in this prophetic tradition. Indeed, some of his disciples and onlookers wonder aloud if he is "one of the prophets." That is because he is constantly railing against those in power—whether it be the power of the Roman occupiers or the powers that be in the religious establishment who collaborate with the occupiers—for their treatment of the poor, the marginalized, the dispossessed, the sick, and the poor. Jesus often mentions the lack of care for "widows and orphans," who are powerless because there is no man in their lives—a man being necessary for social, economic, and political standing in the society. Jesus was always getting into trouble for his prophetic confrontations with the secular and religious powers that be, and indeed it was his critique of—and the potential for his leading a rebellion against—those powers that got him crucified.

For Jews who take the prophetic tradition seriously, and for Christians who seek (at least in theory) to be Christlike, one has to wonder what prophetic messages God would want uttered in His name in this day and time. Certainly the cries of the poor, the oppressed, and the marginalized should be heeded by the powers and principalities. But is it too far a stretch to imagine that gay, lesbian, bisexual, and transgender people would be among those for whom God would have us advocate? Would not the God of love want us to plead the case of lesbian, gay, bisexual, and transgender people, even if we have no existential stake in that issue? I believe so.

There is no question that taking such an advocacy role in seeking compassion, fair treatment in the society, and the happiness and legal status of marriage for gay and lesbian people will get such advocates in trouble. Going against the prevailing culture almost always does. But we are in good company. Jesus teaches in the Sermon on the Mount, "Blessed are those who are persecuted for righteousness' sake, for theirs is the kingdom of heaven. Blessed are you when people revile you and persecute you and utter all kinds of evil against you falsely on my account. Rejoice and be glad, for your reward is great in heaven, for in the same way they persecuted the prophets who were before you" (Matthew 5:10–12).

There is much in our religious tradition that calls us to this ministry of advocacy on behalf of lesbian, gay, bisexual, and transgender people and against their oppression, both within religious institutions and in the culture. It seems clear to me that it is not just those directly affected by these issues who are called to that work of advocacy—but rather all who value and seek justice for all. Indeed, we will never achieve fair treatment and justice for lesbian, gay, bisexual, and transgender people until straight people own this as their issue too.

There is no doubt that the civil rights movement of the 1960s gained momentum when white people also began to own the issue of justice for African-Americans. It was an important milestone when white Americans, who seemingly had no stake in the plight of African-Americans, began to march with Dr. King, write letters to Congress demanding an end to Jim Crow laws, and admit to and confront their own collusion in a racist society. It was when white people began to understand that they too were paying a moral price for racism that the majority started to pay attention and to question its own past behavior.

The fact is, lesbian, gay, bisexual, and transgender people will never be a majority. We are a natural minority within the population. We will never garner enough votes to single-handedly bring about the change we seek. We need heterosexual people to stand with us, vote with us, and be a voice for us where we are not yet welcome.

So how does one become an advocate, even a prophet, on behalf of lesbian, gay, bisexual, and transgender people?

I was speaking once at Colby College in Maine. Among the students waiting to chat with me informally after my presentation was one young man. I could tell he was intent on speaking with me personally, despite the late hour and my need to get to bed after a long day. Nothing would dissuade him. He wanted to thank me for helping his younger brother, who is gay and who had drawn much support from things I had written. Then he said to me, "Oh, and by the way, I have an answer to your question."

During my presentation, I had talked about how fortunate I feel to have had the experience of being gay—because it has been my tiny window into what other oppressions are like. I am on the more powerful end of most oppressions: I am white, I'm an American, I am male, I am wealthy by the world's standards, I am educated, I am able-bodied, I am Western. Without great effort on my part, it is difficult to comprehend and understand my own role in racism, sexism, American hegemony and colonialism, first-world oppression of the two-thirds world, and the ways in which I participate in others' oppression. I was trying to make the point that my experience of being gay helped me see and understand the oppression of others, and for that I was grateful. And then, in a much-too-glib and frivolous way, I said to the audience, "I don't know how any of you straight white guys get it!!" And that was the question this young Colby College freshman had an answer for.

"I'll tell you how we get it," he said. "We listen to you. And then we believe you." There it was, plain and brilliantly simple. When you're trying to understand the plight of someone else, when you're trying to understand someone's experience that has never been *your* experience, you begin by truly listening to him and his stories, really listening. And then—and this is key, I think—you *believe* his truth. It may not be your truth, and it may not have been anything you have experienced. But you believe that this is the truth of the other person's experience. And you show infinite respect for him by believing him.

I've stopped quipping about "straight white guys getting it," and I've begun to say that this young, straight man understood fully how to become an advocate for this or any other oppressed group of which he is not a part. He listens deeply to the stories told to him by the "other," and then he believes them. It is, I think, the first step to becoming an advocate.

And so, if you want to understand why a straight person might want to become an advocate for gay and lesbian people, get to know us. Get to know at least one of us well. Listen to our stories, believe our truth. It may not be your truth, but believe it's our truth. Get to know our families. Get close enough to see us at work as faithful partners, loving parents, and contributing members of society. Ask us about our faith. Inquire as to how we seem to have put together our faith and our sexuality. Ask how we have withstood the hatred and prejudice—religious and secular—against us. And then believe us.

I believe that once you have taken the time and trouble to listen to us, to imagine walking in our shoes, and to absorb the truth of our lives, you will no longer see acceptance of us and affirmation of our relationships as our issues alone. They will become your issues. You will understand that "until we are all free, we are none of us free." And you will join us in working for fairness and justice for all.

CHAPTER 3

What's Wrong with Civil Unions?

Recently, two dear friends and longtime partners (twenty-five-plus years) came to New Hampshire to be married. They were limited to a civil union in the state where they reside. On the morning of the wedding, I went with them to our Town Clerk's office to get their marriage license.

It was a mundane task to be accomplished to make everything legal. There was the proof of identity, residence, and age. There was nothing unusual in the information being required, so I wondered why one of the men was taking so long to complete the application. In time, he was finished. The town clerk handed them their completed and certified marriage license and in a cheery, genuine voice said, "Congratulations!"

When we got out to the parking lot, Russ, who had

taken so long to complete the forms, burst into tears. This mundane task had been an unexpectedly moving and powerful experience for him. "I had no idea this would mean so much to me," he said. "I was there, filling out this stupid form with all my information. But it was the government asking me for this information in order to be able to affirm and support my relationship with Dan—the relationship which for twenty-five years the government hasn't acknowledged or even given a damn about. I've been fighting for marriage equality for years, but even I never understood the power and meaning this would have for me, for us. And when the town clerk, the lowly representative of the government, congratulated us and wished us well in our marriage—and genuinely seemed to mean it—I nearly lost it right there! I had no idea!"

Why do we have to talk about gay marriage? Can't gay people just be satisfied and grateful for the gains they have made—and be quiet? Can't they just stop pushing?" You hear things like that from good, tolerant people who have generally gotten used to the idea of gay people wanting their equal rights. While they are somewhat tolerant of these demands, the demand for marriage seems to go too far, to push the envelope in a way that makes people uncomfortable and defensive.

"Don't Ask, Don't Tell," now relegated to its seventeen-year history, was generally a popular policy from its beginning because it put into law the very stance most people felt comfortable with: It's okay to be gay, but for God's sake, don't talk about it! The fact is that such a stance hardly indicates in truth that it's "okay to be gay." One might acknowledge the existence and pervasiveness of cancer, and learn to tolerate its presence, but would never affirm it as something to be desired or respected. But we are talking about people here, not a life-threatening illness.

Some "tolerant" people might even say, in exasperation, "I know you are gay, but do you have to keep rubbing it in my face? Stop flaunting it!" Such sentiments mark only a slight improvement over outright intolerance. Now, to be sure, tolerance is preferable to intolerance, and a "let it be" attitude is certainly much better than violence against lesbian, gay, bisexual, and transgender (LGBT) people. But it's not much of an improvement. To someone like me, on the receiving end of this kind of "tolerance," it still feels abusive and life denying and not a lot different from outright disdain. Perhaps that seems unfair and small-minded to those who say these things, but most gay and lesbian people I know are not willing to live happily with that more subtle form of heterosexism.

The "not wanting to talk about it" and the warning "don't flaunt it" are indications that the tolerance doesn't go very deep. Heterosexual men and women wear wedding bands and introduce each other as husband and wife, yet somehow this doesn't qualify as "flaunting" their heterosexual practices. When a straight man refers to his wife in casual conversation, he's just stating a fact, but when a gay man refers to his partner or (in some places) husband, he's rubbing the world's nose in his private and sexual life.

I attended a conference once on combating homophobia in which the facilitator asked all the participants, whether gay or straight, to introduce themselves by name and then to state boldly, "I'm a gay man" or "I'm a lesbian." He then challenged the participants to avoid saying anything, all day, that would correct this declaration. No mention of who was left at home with the kids, no talk—even at lunch—about what you did over the weekend and with whom, no indication whatsoever that you were *not* gay or lesbian. It was intriguing to watch straight people do the kind of self-censoring and filtering of their conversation that is common to the lives of gay and lesbian people. The heterosexual participants found it both uncomfortable and exhausting. Many commented later on how much energy it took to be constantly monitoring what you were about to say, to make sure you didn't give away your "secret" of being straight. Many wondered how LGBT people do it, day in and day out.

The overall effect of such a self-censoring regime is self-loathing. Every time we do it, we feel "less than." We collaborate with our cultural oppressors every time we short-circuit something we were about to say or change a pronoun to disguise the gender of the person being referred to, and it reinforces and absorbs the inherent dis-crimination. And it feels lousy. I suppose it's not unlike a black man who unenthusiastically adds a "sir" whenever he's talking to a white man. Or like a disabled person who apologizes for the inconvenience of her wheelchair. The culture has subtle (and sometimes not so subtle) ways of enforcing its dominant norms on those who don't fit those norms. And every time it happens, we feel diminished.

Language is important too. To understand that gay marriage is not the same as civil union, we must look at the power of words and what we call things—and people. There was a time when "Negro" was a step forward from using the *n* word. Then, as Negroes began to assert their own dignity and worth, their language used to describe themselves also changed. "Negro" gave way to a number of other words of self-description—"black," "Afro-American," "African-American"—each with its own history and connotations. White Americans grew impatient with their black brothers and sisters, and they complained that they didn't know what the proper moniker was anymore. But those white Americans who really cared about black people struggled to keep up, because it mattered to them what black Americans themselves wanted to be called. If you care about someone, nothing is more important than calling him by his preferred name. From Adam's naming of the animals in Genesis, naming has been an important task.

Language and naming are important to the gay community too. As the budding civil rights movement for homosexuals progressed, the words used to name ourselves changed too. "Gay" came to be the preferred term. Heterosexual people wondered what was wrong with "homosexual."

For starters, it's a medical term and feels like a diagnosis. In 1972, a gay psychiatrist named John Pryor stood in front of the American Psychiatric Association national conference, wearing a Richard Nixon Halloween mask and a wig, and declared, "I am a psychiatrist. And I am gay." He then went on to make the case for homosexuality *not* being in the *Diagnostic and Statistical Manual of Mental Disorders*, and within a short time homosexuality was removed from that list of illnesses. "Homosexual" feels cold and clinical.

On the other hand, "gay" feels affirming and positive. It suggests that being homosexual does not necessarily indicate a psychologically disordered, grim, desperate life lived in the shadows or a life more susceptible than that of heterosexuals to addictions and unhappiness. It suggests a life in which joy, happiness, and contentment can abound between those who are erotically and affectionally drawn to people of the same gender. *Within* that same-gender-loving community, further distinctions have been made, identifying the gender of those same-gender-loving people, namely gay men (men who are oriented toward men) and lesbians (women who are oriented toward women). While the general descriptor "gay" is used for the entire same-gender-loving community, the further descriptors "gay" and "lesbian" have been important to that community, despite the confusion they may produce in those who seek to understand them.

The other shift that such a designation points to is this distinction important to the gay community: being gay is not about what we *do;* it's about who we *are.* It is impossible to overstate the importance of this and the degree to which heterosexual people don't understand it. The word "homosexual" seems to define us solely in terms of the gender of the person we're sexually intimate with. There is much more to us than our sexuality. And besides, many gay and lesbian people—some very young, and some very old—have *never* been sexually intimate with anyone of the same gender, yet they know and understand themselves as gay. It's more about the lens through which we see the world. It's about our history of being an oppressed and discriminated-against minority. It's about the culture that colludes to make us feel unworthy, immoral, and dirty. Every person, gay or straight, encounters the world in a particular body, with a particular sexual orientation. It affects every interaction, whether with the same or the opposite gender. That orientation affects every relationship, every encounter with another person, even if the relationship is not romantic or sexual in any way. It affects the chemistry of a relationship and the nature of the human interaction. And that is true whether or not a person has ever "acted on" the same-sex attractions he or she has felt.

It could be argued, of course, that the word "heterosexual" is just as demeaning to straight people as the word "homosexual" is to gay people, reducing them to this one characteristic. The difference is that "heterosexual" has never been used as a "diagnosis" against straight people. Homosexuality, until 1973, was considered by psychiatrists to be a clinical disorder. It was a diagnosis. "Heterosexual," on the other hand, has always been an objective adjective to describe a "normal" person. It simply does not carry the emotional wallop and psychological or medical baggage that "homosexual" does.

This use of "homosexual" and its reduction of people to what they do with their genitals are exacerbated by this question of "acting on" one's feelings. Some religious groups now attempt to sound gay-positive by saying that being gay is not a problem—*as long as* you don't act on those attractions. This reduces being gay to gay sexual acts. Not only is it an affront to those of us who are gay; it is simply silly.

If my church says it's okay to be gay as long as I don't act on my attractions to people of the same sex, when does the forbidden activity begin? If I live with another man but never touch him, is that okay? If we share a bedroom but sleep in separate twin beds, is that okay? If we share a bed but never touch each other, is that okay? Are we "gay" yet?! How about if I only hold his hand? Only touch him above the waist? Only tell him I love him, but never act that love out with my body? At what point are we "gay"?

I would argue that I am "gay" all the time, waking and sleeping. I am not just gay when I am making love to someone of the same gender, but all the time. In my experience, it is men who generally engage in this kind of reductionism. Perhaps that is because men are more likely to separate their emotions from their actions, even their lovemaking. Men seem more able and more willing than women to have sex without recognizing and acknowledging their feelings or emotions. In my experience, it is men who when confronted by someone gay immediately start thinking of physical acts.

The fact of the matter is that I am "acting gay" all the time—most of which does not involve any sort of intimate activity. "Gay" is who I am, a whole constellation of ways in which I see and engage the world. It is not merely how—and with whom—I employ my genitals for sexual satisfaction and mutual pleasure.

Many heterosexuals did (and still do) find the word "gay" irritating. "Why did they have to go and 'ruin' a perfectly good word? It used to be that a gathering or party could be described as gay, and everyone knew that a good time was had by all. But now these homosexuals have commandeered this word for themselves. How dare they use such a positive word to describe this 'lifestyle' which is sad at best, and immoral and debased at worst!"

This claiming of the word "gay" is more powerful and more important than straight people usually understand. Its introduction represented a coming-out for same-gender-oriented people everywhere, whether they used it to describe themselves or not. It cast their condition in a positive light, even if society was not yet ready to treat them positively. Indeed, "gay" represented a kind of quiet naming revolution against centuries of oppression and became a defiant sort of self-assertion. The efficacy of that self-assertion was evidenced in the dominant culture's resistance to it. We, the gay community, knew we had hit a nerve, and we knew that its gradual acceptance meant progress. It seems like a little thing, but I can remember vividly when *The New York Times* made the editorial decision to change its references from "homosexual" to "gay." These things matter to victims of oppression. "Gay" matters to us.

Of course, "gay" didn't remain sufficient for long. "Gay" women spoke up and pointed out that the experience of homosexual women was in some important ways distinctly different from that of gay men, not the least of which was their double discrimination as gay *and* female in a dominant culture that was heterosexual and male. And so we had the "gay and lesbian" community. Then bisexuals and transgender people spoke up about their own, different experience. The LGBT community was named.

I have observed another subtle, nearly unnoticed shift within the LGBT community. If my memory serves me correctly, we started out as the GLBT community. Over time, gay men (at least some of them) wanted to acknowledge and honor the special, double-barreled discrimination experienced by their lesbian sisters by naming them first in the acronym. Almost without anyone noticing, the GLBT community morphed into the LGBT community.

All of this may seem to the heterosexual reader terribly picky and insignificant—and irrelevant to the debate about marriage equality. But I assure you it is important. Naming is powerful. It sets the terms of the debate. It matters to those being named, and judging by the resistance to it, it matters to those who haven't a clue about why it's important.

"Why can't homosexuals be satisfied with civil unions? Why do they want the word 'marriage' too?" Everyone knows what marriage is, the commitments it implies, the respect and deference it commands. But who knows what a civil union is, or what it means?

In states that have lawful civil unions for same-gender couples, numerous problems have arisen because of this confusion. Legally joined partners in a civil union have found themselves in emergency rooms, one of them bleeding profusely or doubled over in stomach pain, trying to explain their rights to hospital staff who are insisting that "only family" is allowed in the room with the patient. That is no time to be explaining the rights and responsibilities of those joined in a civil union. A simple "We are married" takes care of the confusion. The experience with civil unions so far is that hospitals, law enforcement officers, lawyers, social agencies, nursing homes, and the general public simply do not understand civil unions and do not know what rights are guaranteed by them.

When my husband and I were joined in a legal civil union (prior to our being married under New Hampshire's marriage equality law), we often joked about how to describe ourselves. We would laughingly say, "We were unionized." Now that we are legally married, it is clear to anyone who will listen. "He's my husband." Marriage is the culture's way of applauding and supporting relationships that foster stability and security—not just for the couple, but for the society. However we might be living up to our commitments, when we say we are married, people know that we have made commitments to each other, that we take them seriously, and that we have taken on all the responsibilities of marriage and expect all the rights accorded to married couples. At the moment, that is true for the State of New Hampshire but not the United States of America. And that's why marriage equality matters, and why the *word* matters.

To heterosexual opponents of marriage equality, I would ask: If the word "marriage" shouldn't matter all that much to us, as long as we get all the privileges of marriage, then why don't we *all* change our permanent and legal relationships to civil unions? Let's have the State authorize *only* civil unions, changing everyone's legal status to that of a civil union. How would formerly "married" people feel about now having their status changed to a civil union? They would probably feel "second-class," which is precisely the point the gay community is trying to make.

"Separate but equal" has never worked very well, especially for the minority who is the target of the separation. We saw how it worked in racial segregation. Even after slaves were freed in the Emancipation Proclamation, look how long it took us to grant real and meaningful equality to African-Americans. I would argue that that task is still not completed. But surely we learned that "separate but equal" schools, movie theaters, fraternities, and drinking fountains did not serve any of us well. We were equal in name, but the reality was that some were more equal than others. We claim "liberty and justice for all," but our history shows that "separate but equal" undermines any efforts to make that goal a reality.

Neither does "separate but equal" work when it comes to the State's authorization and recognition of relationships. If the purpose and intention of permanent, committed relationships are the same, whether between opposite-gender or same-gender partners, then why not the same legal status and name? Does anyone really believe that a civil union is the same as a marriage? Does anyone really believe it confers the same societal acknowledgment and support? Does anyone believe it doesn't bestow second-class status?

Our intimate and committed relationships are in every way equal in purpose and intention to heterosexual marriages. Marriage is the institution that honors the love between two people and the self-sacrificing commitments they have made to each other and to the wider community. So let's call it what it is: marriage.

CHAPTER 4

Doesn't the Bible Condemn
Homosexuality?

I never missed a single day of Sunday school. Not in thirteen years! I once gave measles to my entire Sunday school class because I didn't tell my mother I was sick on Sunday morning—because I didn't want to mess up my perfect attendance record. I may have given them all measles, but I maintained my perfect attendance!

Children were not the only people in Sunday school in the small, rural church where I grew up. Everyone came at 10:00 on Sunday morning to engage in an hour of Bible study. Worship was at 11:00, but prior to that every member of the church was steeped in the study of the Old and New Testaments. It was the solid foundation upon which our faith—and my faith—were built.

Along with some of the frightening stories in Scripture (for example, God calling upon Abraham to sacrifice his son Isaac and the seemingly astronomical body counts of the dead in the armies who opposed the Israelites and their God Yahweh), there were stories of the limitless love Jesus exhibited for the outcast, the lonely, the poor, the despised, the widowed, and the orphaned. There was talk of a God, whom Jesus called "Father," who loved all of creation, including the oh-so-fallible human beings that God considered to be "children" and "heirs of the Kingdom."

I had a difficult time reconciling the two visions of God. By the time I was in high school, that difficulty led to considerable skepticism on my part. I began to ask a lot of questions, culminating in the conundrum that plagued me the most: If God loves humankind, how can He (at the time, I would have gone along with the male moniker) condemn to everlasting damnation all those who have never heard of Jesus or haven't accepted him as their Lord and Savior?

When posing that question to my elders, I was told, "You know, there are some questions you simply shouldn't ask!" Even at the ripe old age of seventeen, I knew there were questions that were not easy to answer, even questions that had no answer, but I thought there was no question that shouldn't be asked.

If Scripture couldn't stand up to the scrutiny of a seventeen-year-old, what good was it to anybody? Thus began my search for a way both to honor Scripture and to hold it accountable for making sense.

.   .   .

How are we to regard the Bible as a whole? It's the first question we must ask, and the answer we give is an important one, guiding the reading and understanding of any particular text. This question has been not only the source of much debate through the centuries but even the cause of bloodshed.

I would argue that in order to interpret any passage in Scripture, we must employ three lenses: the Scripture itself; the tradition of how the Church has interpreted that Scripture over the centuries; and reason, that is, the use of our own God-given intellect and learning, up to and including how modern knowledge, science, psychology, and reason inform our understanding of the issues being addressed by the Scripture. But first, and always first, is the Scripture itself.

Be assured, I believe the Bible to be the Word of God—but not the "words" of God. That is, I do not believe that the Bible was dictated by God and written down by scribes of one sort or another, unmediated by the scribes' own life experiences, culture, religious belief, and context.

I believe that the Bible is many accounts, by many writers, over a thousand years, of their experience of the Living God. Their accounts were heard (more often than read) as an experiential guide on how one accesses God (or how God accesses humankind) and discerns God's will. The Bible is a collection of firsthand encounters with God, as experienced through the faithful (and sometimes unfaithful) people of God—from the Israelites in the Hebrew

Scriptures (somewhat condescendingly referred to by Christians as the "Old" Testament) and the Christians of the early Church in the "New" Testament.

As such, it is the place we always begin. In reading these holy texts, we learn the ways that people of faith have historically come to know God and God's will. They are enormously instructive, and over several millennia these texts have served as a guide for pilgrims of faith in their encounters with the Living God.

Some of these texts are history; some are poetry. Some are fables and myths, meant to teach an important truth. Some are personal accounts of individuals, and some are communal accounts of a nation. All are set in a particular historical and cultural context. And *context* is the central key in understanding these texts and the prism through which we accomplish the all-important task of determining whether the wisdom contained therein is applicable to all people for all time.

Let's take an example of the importance of context, drawn from Daniel Helminiak's 1994 book, *What the Bible Really Says About Homosexuality.* Let's say it's the year 3000 and the game of baseball has been lost to us. No one plays it; no one even knows about this popular sport that disappeared centuries ago.

Then someone picks up a novel written in the year 2000 and finds a character described as being "out in left field." The reader in the year 3000 would assume he knows what that means. After all, he knows what "left" is, and he knows what a "field" is! But unless he knew about and understood the game of baseball, he would not actually understand what the author was trying to communicate. He wouldn't know that most batters are right-handed, tending to hit balls into the left field of play. And he wouldn't know that the players known as left fielders tended to stay far back in the field of play, to be in a better position to catch high-flying balls into left field, but distancing them from the rest of the players. And he wouldn't know that being "out in left field" had become a metaphor for being detached, isolated, out of the mainstream, and even a little weird. The modern reader would know the literal meaning of the words but would completely miss the true meaning of the author's words.

And so it is with reading Scripture. We may know the actual (and current) meaning of the words, but without understanding the context and figurative meaning of the words and phrases at the time they were written, we may in fact misunderstand the author's intent.

Indeed, much of the biblical scholarship of the latter half of the twentieth century has been concerned with understanding the contexts in which the Scriptures were written. Scholars have researched and discovered much about the culture, science, knowledge, biases, and pressing issues in the societies of the ancient world—both within the Hebrew and early Christian communities and in the hostile, threatening, and pagan cultures that surrounded them. To go back to our analogy, scholars have been learn-

ing about the various games of "baseball" operative at the
time the Scriptures were written, with the purpose of better understanding the meaning of those words.

So, first and foremost, in reading texts from the Bible, we
must ask, "What did these words mean to their author?"
and "What did these words mean to the community for
which they were written?" Once the context has been
understood, we ask the question, "Is the message of this
text eternally binding on all people of faith, or has something changed in the context between then and now that
renders this text 'culturally bound' and not applicable in
the same way to our current situation, given the knowledge
and understandings of the present time?"

Not even the strictest fundamentalist or biblical literalist gives the same authority and moral weight to every
word of Scripture. Few of us would hold Paul's injunc-
tion against women appearing in church with their heads
uncovered to have the same moral weight as Jesus's injunc-
tion to forgive our enemies. (Although recent scholarship
by Sarah Ruden and others shows that even Paul was far
more egalitarian and far less misogynist than a cursory
reading might first suggest!) Few of us are willing to be
bound by all the commands given to us in the biblical
text; otherwise, we would give all we have to the poor to
follow Christ, redistribute all the land every fifty years,
refuse to charge any interest on our loans and investments,
share our worldly possessions communally as did the early
Church, and refuse to support our nation's defense budget

in accord with Jesus's commandment not to resist evil. We have come to understand certain things as acceptable in the biblical culture and time but not in our own—among other things, polygamy and slavery, which few Christians would promote despite their acceptability in biblical times. As we approach the biblical texts about homosexuality, we must not conveniently change our stance to one of asserting that every word of Scripture is inerrantly true and universally binding on all people for all time.

Understanding Scripture in its contexts is no easy task, and it is fraught with potential misuse. All readers of Scripture are subject to self-deception—that is, the temptation to interpret the Scriptures in a way that satisfies our own selfish desires and biases, rather than hearing the truth of the passage that may challenge, condemn, and call into question those desires and biases. That is why Scripture must always be studied and understood *in community*. The temptation is too great to interpret Scripture in our own image to attempt it alone. One must always be subject to the larger community's understandings to guard against only hearing what one wants to hear.

Part of the community whose voice needs to be considered is that of tradition—that is, what has been said over the years about any given passage of Scripture. We, in the present time, are not the only ones who have struggled with these passages, and our own understanding needs to be informed by the larger community of the faithful in the past.

We need to use our own reason and experience in interpreting these passages of Scripture. Our knowledge of science, psychology, and modern scholarly understandings needs to inform our approach to these passages. Our knowledge about common allusions in Scripture—from leprosy to demon possession, from conception and birth to race and gender realities—will inform our interpretation based on new findings from the secular realm.

These lenses—Scripture, tradition, and reason—will allow us to look clearly at the seven verses of Scripture traditionally thought to be associated with the issue of homosexuality. To switch metaphors, Scripture, tradition, and reason are the classic "three-legged stool" of authority used in historical Anglicanism and many other religious traditions.

It is important to mention that many Christians, myself included, do not believe that God stopped revealing God's self with the closing of the canon of Scripture (those books officially included in the body of writings that would be designated as the "Bible"). Some would argue that God said everything God needed and wanted to say by the end of the first century of the Common Era (a less condescending way of referring to that time since the birth of Christ, "common" to both Jews and Christians). While Christians who favor a more literalist reading of Scripture would not blatantly put it quite this way, they seem to posit a God who, when the Scriptures were "finished," almost bade the world a fond farewell and went off to some beautiful part of His creation (the Bahamas, Patagonia, Nepal), leaving us to our own devices, given that everything had been said that needed to be said. I don't believe that for a minute, and to be honest, most of these same biblical literalists posit a God who cares about our every move and seeks to guide us along our way. This understanding of God as being active in the creation—not just in biblical times, but to this very day—is at the heart of Christianity.

In John's Gospel, which is largely made up of the conversation Jesus has with his disciples at the Last Supper, Jesus says: "I still have many things to say to you, but you cannot bear them now. When the Spirit of truth comes, he will guide you into all the truth" (16:12–13a). I take this to mean that Jesus is saying to the disciples, "Look, for a bunch of uneducated and rough fishermen, you haven't done too badly. In fact, you will do amazing things with the rest of your lives. But don't think for a minute that God is done with you—or done with believers who will come after you. There is much more that God wants to teach you, but you cannot handle it right now. So I will send the Holy Spirit, who will lead you into that new truth."

I hope it is with great shame that we remember that the Church used Scripture to justify slavery until the mid-nineteenth century, when the Church acknowledged that it had gotten this all wrong and began to change itself and the culture into a less oppressive, more compassionate community. Was that not the Spirit leading us to a new truth about people of color and the sin of racism? For centuries, and still to this day in some quarters of Christianity, Judaism, and Islam, Scripture has been used to denigrate and subjugate women. But many of us have come to know the error of those ways as we experience the gifts for ministry that women have been given and recognize God's call to women to leadership in our religious communities. Is that not the Spirit leading the Church to say "we got it wrong" all these years?

And now, in these times, we are swept up in the holy chaos of asking, "Could we, people of faith, have been just as wrong about lesbian, gay, bisexual, and transgender people? Might it be the Holy Spirit leading us to a new truth about homosexuality? Do we have the courage to admit we were wrong all these years? Are we open to being led by the Spirit to a new place?"

I believe we have been wrong. And I believe it *is* the Holy Spirit leading us to this new understanding. And yet we have these seven texts in Scripture with which we must deal. We cannot sweep them aside merely because we don't like them. We must understand them in their contexts and see if there is a faithful way forward, following the Spirit's lead, in learning this new truth.

"Homosexuality" in Leviticus

First, and most famous, of the scriptural texts used to condemn homosexuality are the two references in the Holiness Code of Leviticus: "You shall not lie with a male as with a woman; it is an abomination" (18:22); and "If a man lies with a male as with a woman, both of them have committed an abomination; they shall be put to death; their blood is upon them" (20:13).

The context of these two passages is the holiness and purity codes recorded for the people of Israel—rules enumerated to define what was clean and unclean before God, as well as what set the Hebrew people apart from their heathen neighbors who worshipped gods other than the one true God. These holiness and purity codes take as their premise the notion that there is a natural or normal state of things, and because it is "natural" or "normal," it must be God's will. And therefore any deviation is by definition deviant, not normal, unclean, and against God's will. Because women spend only a portion of the month menstruating, their "normal" state is between menstrual cycles, and therefore they are "unclean" during menstruation. Because eyesight is "normal," blindness is abnormal, and therefore unclean. Because ambulatory movement is "normal," lameness is abnormal and unclean—which is why lameness was an impediment to being a priest in ancient Israel.

Similarly, it is "natural" and "normal" for men to desire women, and therefore men who have sexual relations with other men are not "normal" and indeed are acting "against their nature." It never occurred to the ancient Israelites that a man might naturally be affectionally, erotically drawn toward other men. And no mention is made at all in the Hebrew Scriptures of women having sexual relations with other women. The notion that a certain small minority of the population would be so inclined toward people of the same gender simply was not countenanced in the ancient Jewish mind. Because everyone was understood to be "heterosexual" (presumably, this word did not even exist at the time, since it only has meaning in contrast to "homosexual"), any same-gender sexual activity was unclean and prohibited as acting against one's own nature. Indeed, it would have been an "abomination" to God and God's natural order.

This is an important point, difficult for the modern mind to grasp: homosexuality as a sexual orientation was unknown to the ancient mind. Let me be clear: intimate physical contact between people of the same gender was not unknown, of course, but *everyone* who engaged in it was presumed to be heterosexual. Therefore, any man who lay with another man as with a woman was considered a heterosexual man acting against his true nature.

The psychological construct of a homosexual orientation was not posited until the late nineteenth century—the notion that a certain minority of humankind is affectionally oriented toward people of the same gender, rather than the opposite gender. For people so oriented, intimate physical contact with people of the opposite gender would be "against their nature." There was no question that same-gender intimate behavior existed (and was therefore prohibited), but there was no understanding that such same-gender attraction might be "in the nature" of a certain minority of people. Such a possibility was simply never contemplated by the ancient mind.

To understand this a bit better, think of the world prior to the voyages of Columbus, Magellan, and other explorers of the New World. The paradigm of a flat earth prevailed, and we would not expect pre–New World thinking to take into account the reality of a round earth. Similarly, prior to the work of Freud, Jung, and countless others in the "new" field of psychology, the notion of demon possession was quite common in explaining phenomena now regarded as mental illness. We are mostly untroubled when we read in Scripture about those "possessed by a demon," understanding in our minds that this was probably some sort of mental disturbance, inexplicable to the people of biblical times.

So in saying that sexual orientation was unknown in the ancient mind, we are trying to imagine the world before there was any understanding of the possibility that some human beings would *naturally* be erotically drawn to a person of the same gender, rather than the opposite gender. There was no question raised in anyone's mind that all human beings were naturally attracted to people of the opposite gender, and therefore those engaging in same-gender behavior were operating outside the bounds of their nature. Such a flagrant violation of that nature was prohibited.

And so these verses from the Leviticus Holiness Code must be read in the context of the assumption that everyone was heterosexual by nature, and acting contrary to that was not "normal," and therefore outside the will of the Creator.

In practice, we modern-day Christians have regarded most of the injunctions in the Holiness Codes of Leviticus and Deuteronomy as culturally bound to the ancient times of the Hebrews—but not binding on us. These same purity codes forbid eating shellfish, planting a field with two different kinds of seeds, or wearing simultaneously two kinds of cloth. They would prohibit us from ordaining to the priesthood any handicapped person—not to mention women. We cannot, then, isolate these passages about homosexual acts and impute to them the kind of enduring authority that we ascribe to nothing before or after them. One has to wonder why the biblical literalists who cite this passage against homosexuality don't seem to go all the way and advocate, like Leviticus, for death as the punishment for homosexual behavior! We cannot have it both ways.

One other guiding principle in these codes that I presume most modern-day Christians and Jews would not espouse is the bias against women. Women are generally regarded as problematic and less worthy and more unclean than men. A man who had a discharge of semen was ritually unclean until sunset, but a woman who menstruated was unclean for a week. When a woman gave birth to a boy, she was unclean for a week, but when she gave birth to a girl, she was unclean for twice as long! I would maintain that part of what made the sin of a man lying "with a male as with a woman" so abominable was the scandal of the noble, privileged, favored male of the species giving up that privilege to take on the role of the less clean, less noble, certainly less privileged female. Indeed it is not extraneous to note that during wartime, a not uncommon practice in the ancient Middle East was for the soldiers of a victorious army to anally rape the captured male enemies. Nothing could symbolize the contempt for and domination over the defeated enemy like raping them—that is, to treat them like women. Those so treated would not soon forget their humiliation and shame. One man using another man as he might use a woman would be not just an act of physical violence but an offense against his very being as a man. Nothing could be worse. So in this context, these injunctions are not surprising.

Finally, there is the context of the "science" of conception of that time. Male sperm was thought to contain all things necessary for procreation. Women contributed nothing but a place for the nascent life to incubate. Therefore, the "spilling of seed" (sperm) on the ground was a kind of abortion, the killing of life. This "scientific" understanding led to other proscriptions in the Holiness Code. Male masturbation is condemned. And the so-called sin of Onan was also condemned. Onan was a heterosexual man who withdrew from intercourse with his wife before ejaculation, spilling his seed on the ground instead of depositing it in his wife's womb. And God strikes him dead.

Add to this the ancient Israelites' need to grow the population. Upon their return from slavery in Egypt, they were surrounded by hostile cultures eager to destroy the invaders who had returned to their "promised land." The Israelites needed to populate their nation in order to withstand the challenge to their presence. For a man to spill his seed on the ground rather than grow more babies was a sin not only against God but against the nation.

Oddly enough, we have relaxed these "rules" against a man "spilling his seed" through masturbation and birth control, yet we hold on to a man "shall not lie with a male as with a woman" as if it were eternally binding on believers. Such an inconsistency simply does not make sense.

Given these changes in our modern understandings and contexts, it is no longer appropriate for us to condemn men who have intimate sexual relationships with other men based on this proscription in the Leviticus Holiness Code. Either *all* of these proscriptions must be eliminated as binding on us, or *all* of them must be adhered to. Biblical literalists cannot have it both ways, picking and choosing which proscriptions will still be enforced as eternally binding and which may be casually tossed aside or explained away.

"Homosexuality" in Sodom and Gomorrah

Now we move on to Sodom and Gomorrah, the infamous cities of homosexual sin. Or is that their sin? Certainly, that is how tradition has passed them on to us—even giving us a name (sodomites) for the unspeakable sin and those who commit it. Because we come to this story with so many preconceptions, it might be best to review what the text actually says:

Genesis 19

The two angels came to Sodom in the evening, and Lot was sitting in the gateway of Sodom. When Lot saw them, he rose to meet them, and bowed down with his face to the ground. He said, "Please, my lords, turn aside to your servant's house and spend the night, and wash your feet; then you can rise early and go on your way." They said, "No; we will spend the night in the square." But he urged them strongly; so they turned aside to him and entered his house; and he made them a feast, and baked unleavened bread, and they ate. But before they lay down, the men of the city, the men of Sodom, both young and old, all the people to the last man, surrounded the house; and they called to Lot, "Where are the men who came to you tonight? Bring them out to us, so that we may know them." Lot went out of the door to the men, shut the door after him, and said, "I beg you, my brothers, do not act so wickedly. Look, I have two daughters who have not known a man; let me bring them out to you, and do to them as you please; only do nothing to these men, for they have come under the shelter of my roof." But they replied, "Stand back!" And they said, "This fellow came here as an alien, and he would play the judge! Now we will deal worse with you than with them." Then they pressed hard against the man Lot, and came near the door to break it down. But the men inside reached out their hands and brought Lot into the house with them, and shut the door. And they struck with blindness the men who were at the door of the house, both small and great, so that they were unable to find the door.

Sodom and Gomorrah Destroyed

Then the men said to Lot, "Have you anyone else here? Sons-in-law, sons, daughters, or anyone you have in the city—bring them out of the place. For we are about to destroy this place, because the outcry against its people has become great before the LORD, and the LORD has sent us to destroy it." So Lot went out and said to his sons-in-law, who were to marry his daughters, "Up, get out of this place; for the LORD is about to destroy the city." But he seemed to his sons-in-law to be jesting.

When morning dawned, the angels urged Lot, saying, "Get up, take your wife and your two daughters who are here, or else you will be consumed in the punishment of the city." But he lingered; so the men seized him and his wife and his two daughters by the hand, the LORD being merciful to him, and they brought him out and left him outside the city. [1–16]

In comprehending the meaning of this passage of Scripture, most modern Old Testament scholars agree that our traditional interpretation of this story may be misguided and that the point of the story was Sodom's violation of the rather strict and universally acknowledged norms of hospitality—a code of ethics one still finds in Middle Eastern cultures today. This unwritten but fiercely practiced code of hospitality was a foundation of civil society in biblical times. The desert is a harsh environment for travelers, and to deny hospitality to a stranger in such a setting was seen to be the height of cruelty.

When the two men are welcomed into Lot's house, local men bang on the door and demand, "Where are the men who came to you tonight? Bring them out to us, so that we may know them." There is some debate about the word "know" here. Most scholars would agree that it has the sexual meaning here, but it is very clear that we are talking about homosexual rape, a violent act of aggression—and clearly something we would all condemn and deem worthy of God's punishment.

And just in case you were not convinced of my characterization of the antiwoman bias before, listen to Lot's proposed solution to this dilemma: "I beg you, my brothers, do not act so wickedly." He then offers his two virgin daughters to be abused by these townsmen instead, saying that these strangers should not be treated in such a violent way. That passage alone should cure anyone from wanting to quote this story as one with lasting authority and worthy of emulation.

A similar story in Judges 19 has the host offer the men his own virgin daughter and his guest's concubine—the latter of whom is abused and "wantonly raped." By morning she is dead:

Judges 19

When the old man looked up and saw the wayfarer in the open square of the city, he said, "Where are you going and where do you come from?" He answered him, "We are passing from Bethlehem in Judah to the remote parts of the hill country of Ephraim, from which I come. I went to Bethlehem in Judah; and I am going to my home. Nobody has offered to take me in. We your servants have straw and fodder for our donkeys, with bread and wine for me and the woman and the young man along with us. We need nothing more." The old man said, "Peace be to you. I will care for all your wants; only do not spend the night in the square." So he brought him into his house, and fed the donkeys; they washed their feet, and ate and drank.

Gibeah's Crime

While they were enjoying themselves, the men of the city, a depraved lot, surrounded the house, and started pounding on the door. They said to the old man, the master of the house, "Bring out the man who came into your house, so that we may have intercourse with him." And the man, the master of the house, went out to them and said to them, "No, my brothers, do not act so wickedly. Since this man is my guest, do not do this vile thing. Here are my virgin daughter and his concubine; let me bring them out now. Ravish them and do whatever you want to them; but against this man do not do such a vile thing." But the men would not listen to him. So the man seized his concubine, and put her out to them. They wantonly raped her, and abused her all through the night until the morning. And as the dawn began to break, they let her go. As morning appeared, the woman came and fell down at the door of the man's house where her master was, until it was light.

In the morning her master got up, opened the doors of the house, and when he went out to go on his way, there was his concubine lying at the door of the house, with her hands on the threshold. "Get up," he said to her, "we are going." But there was no answer. Then he put her on the donkey; and the man set out for his home. [17–28]

Even by the *internal* standards of the Scriptures themselves, a condemnation of same-gender intimate relationships is not the point of the story. The prophet Ezekiel compares the sins of Jerusalem with those of Sodom, which he says had "pride, excess of food, and prosperous ease, but did not aid the poor and needy" (Ezekiel 16:49). No mention of homosexuality being the problem here. The towns of Sodom and Gomorrah, which were an ancient version of wealthy, gated communities, had canceled the law of hospitality to keep strangers from visiting, seeing their wealth, and potentially returning to plunder that wealth. This was the point even Ezekiel drew from the story.

Indeed, Jesus's only reference to the notorious town indicates that he also understood that Sodom's infamy came from its inhospitality. Jesus instructs his disciples that if they go into a town and they are not welcomed, they should shake the dust from their feet and go on to another, knowing "on that day it will be more tolerable for Sodom than for that town" (Luke 10:13). No mention of homosexuality here, even by Jesus. Sodom's sin is one of inhospitality and injustice.

Whatever else one makes of this story, it cannot be used to decry loving, committed, lifelong-intentioned, monogamous relationships between two people of the same gender. It is simply not about that kind of relationship. The story is about homosexual rape, and like any rape it is an act of violence and power, not an act of intimacy and love. In short, the story of Sodom and Gomorrah, and all references to it elsewhere in Scripture, provide no guidance for modern-day believers about the morality or immorality of same-gender-loving people. It simply does not offer an answer to the questions we are asking.

"Homosexuality" in the Gospels

What does Jesus say about homosexuality? Absolutely nothing.

Jesus is not recorded as having said anything related to intimate sexual relationships between people of the same gender. One has to wonder, if homosexuality is such a heinous sin against God, why does Jesus himself never refer to it? One cannot extrapolate affirmation of such relationships from that silence, but still, why no mention of an issue now causing entire churches to split?

Some conservatives argue that Jesus's silence is taken to mean that he was offering no changes to the attitudes and values of the Hebrew Scriptures and their proscriptions. I would argue that such an interpretation is as extravagant and erroneous an extrapolation as would be the inference that Jesus affirmed such behavior. What I think we can safely and responsibly conclude from Jesus's silence is that he was silent on the issue.

Saint Paul's Letter to the Romans

Passages in Paul's epistles to the Romans and the Corinthians, as well as a passage from 1 Timothy, are cited by the tradition as condemning homosexuality. A closer look suggests some questions about that traditional understanding:

> Ever since the creation of the world his eternal power and divine nature, invisible though they are, have been understood and seen through the things he has made. So they are without excuse; for though they knew God, they did not honour him as God or give thanks to him, but they became futile in their thinking, and their senseless minds were darkened. Claiming to be wise, they became fools; and they exchanged the glory of the immortal God for images resembling a mortal human being or birds or four-footed animals or reptiles.
>
> Therefore God gave them up in the lusts of their hearts to impurity, to the degrading of their bodies among themselves, because they exchanged the truth about God for a lie and worshipped and served the creature rather than the Creator, who is blessed for ever! Amen.

For this reason God gave them up to degrading passions. Their women exchanged natural intercourse for unnatural, and in the same way also the men, giving up natural intercourse with women, were consumed with passion for one another. Men committed shameless acts with men and received in their own persons the due penalty for their error.

And since they did not see fit to acknowledge God, God gave them up to a debased mind and to things that should not be done. [Romans 1:20–28]

The Romans passage states that God has turned his back on the ungodly and wicked—most especially those who have given up the one true God for idols. Once again, we must ask the question of context. This passage must be read as part of Paul's general observations and admonishments to the Christians living in Rome. Paul is making the point that Jew and Gentile alike need the Gospel, since *all* are unrighteous and in need of God's saving grace. In particular, he is singling out the misguided practice of idolatry, rampant in the ancient world and contrary to God's will, in which "they exchanged the glory of the immortal God for images resembling a mortal human being or birds or four-footed animals or reptiles." In response to their devotion to idols, says Paul, "God gave them up to degrading passions."

Paul would have been very aware that some idolatrous cults practiced temple prostitution as one of their devotional activities. Temple prostitutes were used for sexual acts—by both men and women—as a symbol of devotion to the idol. It is not clear that this is what Paul was referring to, but it is a practice that would have been familiar to him and denounced by him.

Note that these same-gender acts are a result of idolatry, not the cause of God's anger. Once again, as in the Old Testament, when Paul uses the word "nature," he "apparently refers only to homosexual acts indulged in by those he considered to be otherwise heterosexually inclined; acts which represent a voluntary choice to act contrary to their ordinary sexual appetite."* Paul is referring to people who have "exchanged" or "giv[en] up" their true—and therefore heterosexual—nature. The words "exchanged" and "gave up" clearly indicate that these were people presumed to be heterosexual by "nature" who were turning their backs on their true nature.

Finally, just following this passage (in chapter 2), Paul chastises his readers for any sort of judgmentalism on their parts: "Therefore you have no excuse, whoever you are, when you judge others; for in passing judgment on another you condemn yourself, because you, the judge, are doing the very same things" (Romans 2:1). While Paul has harsh words for idolaters, he seems quick to point out that judgmentalism is to be avoided. Paul seems to be saying that

---

*John J. McNeill, S.J., *The Church and the Homosexual* (Kansas City, KS: Sheeds Andrews and McMeel, 1976), p. 55.

using his words to judge homosexuals (or anyone else) in our own day would be a grievous error.

In short, we are not certain what sexual practices Paul has in mind in this passage. He simply does not tell us. What *is* clear is that these practices are related to the worship of idols—and clearly not what we are talking about today. Our questions involve a modern understanding of human sexuality in which a small minority of people—by their nature—are affectionally oriented toward people of the same gender, a concept unknown to the ancient mind. In the contemporary marriage debate, we are talking not about temple prostitutes but about two people of the same gender who are drawn into a faithful, monogamous, lifelong-intentioned relationship. Not much help here on answering the questions about same-gender marriage we are asking.

"Homosexuality" in 1 Corinthians and 1 Timothy

Saint Paul, a Roman citizen and a Jew (before his dramatic conversion on the road to Damascus), was living in a culture where same-gender sexual expression was not unknown. In two of his letters, one to Timothy and the other to the Christian community in Corinth, Paul writes two passages that are traditionally used to condemn homosexuality in modern times. A closer look at those identified as "male prostitutes" and "sodomites" (in the New Revised

Standard Version translation) reveals serious questions about who is being talked about in these passages:

1 Corinthians 6

Do you not know that wrongdoers will not inherit the kingdom of God? Do not be deceived! Fornicators, idolaters, adulterers, male prostitutes, sodomites, thieves, the greedy, drunkards, revilers, robbers— none of these will inherit the kingdom of God. And this is what some of you used to be. But you were washed, you were sanctified, you were justified in the name of the Lord Jesus Christ and in the Spirit of our God. [9–11]

1 Timothy 1

Now we know that the law is good, if one uses it legitimately. This means understanding that the law is laid down not for the innocent but for the lawless and disobedient, for the godless and sinful, for the unholy and profane, for those who kill their father or mother, for murderers, fornicators, sodomites, slave-traders, liars, perjurers, and whatever else is contrary to the sound teaching that conforms to the glorious gospel of the blessed God, which he entrusted to me. [8–11]

In the letter to the Corinthians, amid the list of those who will not inherit the kingdom of God, Paul uses two

Greek words: *malakoi* and *arsenokoitai.* The first is a common Greek word meaning "soft," and elsewhere in Scripture it is used to describe a garment. Nowhere else in Scripture is it used to describe a person. The early Church seems to have understood it as a person with a "soft" or weak morality. Later, it would come to denote (and be translated as) those who engage in masturbation, or "those who abuse themselves." In our own time, with masturbation having been more popularly accepted, this word has often been used to denote homosexuals. All we actually, factually, know about the word is that it meant "soft."

The Greek word *arsenokoitai* is an even greater mystery. It is found nowhere else in Scripture—nor is there any record of its being used in any other contemporaneous text. We have nothing, neither internal to the Scriptures nor external to them, to give us guidance as to its meaning.

When such a mysterious word appears in an ancient text, the translator must do *something* with it. Even with commonly understood words, a translator has choices to make about which English word best communicates the word's meaning. In the case of a completely unknown word like *arsenokoitai,* the danger of mistranslation is heightened. Many translators have chosen to take the two words together, understanding the Greek word for "soft" as applying to the receptive partner in male-to-male anal intercourse, and have taken the *arsenokoitai* to mean the active partner. This is speculation at best.

Others have speculated that this receptive/active relationship applies to a practice (that would have been known to Paul) in which an older man took a teenage boy "under his wing," taught him the ways of the world, and used him sexually. If this were its true meaning, we would all condemn such a practice as child abuse! No one is arguing for acceptance of such a practice.

The same pairing of words is used in Paul's First Letter to Timothy, with no further light being shed on its meaning. Whatever its meaning, there is no reason to believe that homosexual men or women, as we now understand them, are the targets of Paul's condemnations.

Yet we can understand the prejudice and bigotry that have resulted from the ambitious, if erroneous, translations of these words: depending on the translation, the words "pervert," "sodomite," and even "homosexual" have been used. If an unsuspecting believer picks up his Bible and reads the word "homosexual" in one of these passages, the reader assumes that Paul meant what we mean by that word, and the condemnation of homosexuals seems unequivocally clear. The fact is, we can only speculate about what Paul meant in his use of these words. What we do know is that when the meaning of a word or passage is unclear, the translator's own prejudices are apt to play a part in the words used to translate the unknowable meaning of the Greek. Do we really want to base our condemnation of an entire group of people on a shaky translation of an unknowable Greek word? A reasonable person, not to mention a compassionate Christian, would not.

Whatever one makes of these seven passages in Scripture, it seems clear that they must not be used in the service of condemning homosexuality as we know it today. Simply stated, the Bible does not speak to the questions we are asking today about men and women who are affectionally oriented toward people of the same gender. Taken in their own contexts, these texts speak to situations and from understandings different from our own.

Let me be clear. I am not asserting that the Bible speaks affirmatively of same-gender intimate, sexual relationships. All seven of these passages are negative. They simply are not addressing the questions we are asking in light of modern understandings of psychosexual relationships.

There is, however, much in Scripture about compassion for one's fellow human beings, a call for empathy and justice for the marginalized, and a standard of honesty, mutuality, and love in all relationships. In the end, God believes in love. Therefore, I would argue that Scripture gives us great and lasting guidance for the conduct of our relationships, whether they be with strangers, friends, or lifelong partners. But the Bible simply does not offer the wholesale condemnation of the loving relationships of lesbian, gay, bisexual, and transgender people we are told it does.

CHAPTER 5

What Would Jesus Do?

Jesus is real to me.

When I was twenty-two years old and in seminary, I made a visit with fellow seminarians to a dark, dingy apartment on New York's Lower East Side where two monks lived. They belonged to an Italian order, the Little Brothers of Jesus, and were sent two by two to hot spots around the world to make a gentle witness to the people there. These two monks worked "in the world" at a secular job during the day and then maintained a communal life at night.

We went into their tiny room designated as a chapel to celebrate the Communion service. At the end of that service, I remained behind in order to pray. In the presence of these humble, selfless monks, I felt overwhelmingly inadequate to be studying for the priesthood. I knew I could never emulate their humility and selfless service. What am I doing here? I thought. I am completely and utterly unfit and unworthy to be a priest of the Church.

I was kneeling, praying, telling God of my unworthiness. And then it happened. The kind of thing they lock people up in a mental institution for. I became aware of Jesus's presence. I looked up, and there against the wall I saw Jesus. He was hanging on the cross, still alive and breathing. I could see him down to about his knees. I can't explain it, but there he was, alive and in the room with me. I didn't say anything. Neither did he. But I was overcome with the message "You are my beloved. No, you are not worthy, but I am making you worthy. I want you for a priest."

I don't know if it lasted a few seconds or a few minutes. But I knew that I had been visited by the living Christ. And I knew that despite my unworthiness, I was loved beyond anything I could imagine by the God of all that is. Just loved.

As soon as it ended, I immediately started doubting the experience. I looked on the wall for cracks that might suggest the shape of a cross. I thought maybe I was losing my mind. I was afraid to go into the next room, for fear that my face might be noticeably shining, just as Moses's face always shone after talking with the Lord. In fact, no one noticed and the world seemed to be progressing at its regular pace, despite what I had just experienced.

I didn't tell anyone of this experience for nearly twenty

years. It was too private, too crazy, too vulnerable to scrutiny. But there it was, quietly nurturing and supporting me with the knowledge that I was loved by whatever we label as God, that Jesus was alive and real, and that no matter whatever else happened to me, nothing could separate me and God's love for me.

I believe in Jesus. I believe that Jesus was the perfect revelation of God. Not the only revelation of God (what kind of a limited God would that be, if God couldn't reveal God's self in multiple ways?!), but the way in which I have been able to be in relationship to the Living God. As a follower of The Way (as early Christians were known), I'm interested in what Jesus would do when encountering the issues of today—global poverty, environmental degradation, immigration, the growing gap between rich and poor. Christians, quite rightly, ask, "What would Jesus do? What would be the Christlike thing to think? On what basis would we suppose Jesus's attitude toward anything?"

My belief in Jesus Christ is in the context of my understanding of the Trinity—that sacred mystery held by Christians for countless centuries. It claims that our experience of God can happen in an infinite variety of ways but that they tend to group themselves into three categories: our experience of the Creator of all that is (God the Father), God's self-revelation in the life, death, and resurrection of one man at a particular time in human history (God the Son), and our continuing interaction with God through community with one another (God the Holy Spirit). The latter "person" of the Trinity, the Holy Spirit, is the one Jesus promises to send, who will lead the community into all truth. I take that to mean that God did not end God's self-revelation with the closing of the canon of holy Scripture, but rather continues to reveal God's self to us through our interactions with one another and with God.

This is what allows me the freedom to ask "What would Jesus do?" Not that Jesus, the historical figure placed in time, actually faced the issues we face today; but rather that our grounding in a living relationship with God allows us to imagine, in the context of a community with others, what God would have us say, believe, and do in response to new realities that present themselves to us.

What would Jesus do if he found himself in twenty-first-century America, where lesbian, gay, bisexual, and transgender people are experiencing greater and greater acceptance—both by the culture and by people and institutions of faith—and working for their equal protections and rights? What would Jesus think about two men or two women getting married?

Anyone who claims to *know* what God thinks about anything is walking on thin ice. The surer someone is about what God does or does not think, the more skeptical I become. That said, people of faith are asking this question all the time! "What is the godly, Christlike thing to do in this situation?" is another way of meditating on what God thinks about something and what God would have us do.

Such an exercise is what it means to be a person of faith. Religious people are constantly trying to conform their lives to their best understanding of God's will—for the world in general and for them as individuals in that world. We are forever trying to figure out how the choices and situations that face us might be dealt with in a way that reflects the values of the Creator, the incarnated Jesus, and the ongoing revelation of the Holy Spirit. While "What would Jesus do?" (WWJD) has become a cliché, it is, at the end of the day, what we're all trying to figure out.

Well, to be honest, not all of us are asking, "What would Jesus do?" Religious people of all stripes are seeking the right thing to do. For Jews, the will of God is guided by their reading of the Torah, the Writings, and the Prophets, along with the thinking of rabbis and teachers since. Muslims, members of the third major religion tracing itself back to Abraham, would look principally at the life and teaching of the Prophet Muhammad, blessed be He, augmented by the teachings of Moses, Jesus, and other prophets. But I am a Christian, and it is from that perspective that I seek to discern God's will. While I acknowledge and honor other faith traditions and other ways of discerning God's will, I must speak out of the faith I know and experience in my own life.

And how do we go about faithfully, carefully, and prayerfully discerning God's will? Well, faithfully, carefully, and prayerfully! We ask the question "faithfully" by learning what we can from Scripture, being cautious about reading into the text what is not there. And then we ask what implications from Scripture we see that might point us to a modern application of those learnings in a way that is consonant with what we find in the holy texts. We ask the question "What would Jesus do?" and come to our answers "carefully" by remembering that we are only extrapolating the mind of God based on what God has revealed to us in the light of God's revelation in Christ. We are not perfect at it, and we are susceptible to our own biases and hoped-for outcomes—which is why we must always do such extrapolation in the context of the community, which tests and corrects and broadens our personal perceptions. Finally, we ask the question "prayerfully," asking God's assistance in this work, seeking that not our own will "but thine be done." My experience is that when I ask God to be a part of my thinking, I often wind up in a different place than I might have otherwise. This is God's Holy Spirit "lead[ing] us into all truth."

First, let's acknowledge that according to the accounts of the life of Jesus as recorded in the Gospels, Jesus never said anything about sexually intimate relationships between people of the same gender. Nor did he comment on sexual behavior between two people of the same gender. Period. Everything we say about what he might have thought about such relationships is extrapolation from other things he thought, said, and did. But they are not without basis either.

We know, for instance, that Jesus was a champion of the oppressed, the poor, and the marginalized. His sympathy for them came from an attitude of infinite respect for all of God's children, and he seemed to be personally in pain over their suffering. The sick, according to the common understanding, were sick because of their own sins or the sins of their forebears. But Jesus always approached them with compassion—often pronouncing them forgiven of their sins just for good measure (much to the consternation of those who would judge them). Jesus was famous for his daring approach to lepers, seemingly not caring about his own possible infection and defying the rules that isolated lepers from the healthy population, reaching out and touching not only their bodies but their spirits.

The poor had a special place in Jesus's heart, a sure result of his being steeped in the Scriptures of the Judaism on which he was raised. The prophets spoke truth to power and criticized the system that exploited the poor for the benefit of the wealthy and the powerful. Jesus continued in that vein throughout his life and work. Indeed, Jesus saved his most scathing criticism for the powerful of his day who clothed their oppression in religious garb.

He was especially kind to those who were looked down upon by polite society. He was critical of the moral arbiters of his time, condemning their arrogance and judgmental attitude. He understood that the Roman occupiers and their local collaborators exacted a terrible price—financial and human—from the most vulnerable. This was not merely personal injustice but systemic oppression. He was a revolutionary who meant to change the system that oppressed the most vulnerable.

What can we surmise from this? Jesus was consistently

on the side of those who were outcast by society and bore the unfair burden of disdain, discrimination, and prejudice. It is likely that he would look at modern-day lesbian, gay, bisexual, and transgender people and hold real sympathy for them and their plight. He would have understood the implications of a system set up to benefit the heterosexual majority over the homosexual minority. It is hard to imagine Jesus joining in the wholesale discrimination against LGBT people. Isn't it logical that he would be sympathetic to young gay teens who take their own lives rather than live with the stigma attached to their sexual orientation? Would he not be found speaking a word of support, encouragement, and hope to them? Would he not be seeking a change in the hearts of those who treat them as outcasts?

Jesus had an alternative vision of family. The religious Right has "family values" as a centerpiece of its understanding of what God intends for humankind. There is very little in Scripture to back up the notion of a nuclear family, headed by a biological father and mother. Indeed, in addition to calling some of his disciples away from their families to follow him, Jesus had some startling things to say about family and for himself chose a radically different lifestyle.

Jesus, as far as we know, never married—in a culture that virtually required it. We have no record of his ever being sexually intimate with another person. He spent the years of his public ministry in the close company of a "family of choice," both men and women. His closest friends were a group of twelve men with whom he spent virtually every waking minute.

Jesus redefines the meaning of family for himself and for his followers. Once, when he was preaching and teaching, his biological mother and brothers attempted to talk to him:

> Someone told him, "Look, your mother and your brothers are standing outside, wanting to speak to you." But to the one who had told him this, Jesus replied, "Who is my mother, and who are my brothers?" And pointing to his disciples, he said, "Here are my mother and my brothers! For whoever does the will of my Father in heaven is my brother and sister and mother." (Matthew 12:47–50)

These seemingly harsh words point to a redefinition of family, based not on biology but on shared interests and values. Jesus seems to be saying that relationships by blood count for little compared with those familial relationships formed by intention, based on common beliefs and values.

What can we surmise from this? Jesus would not be shocked by or opposed to new definitions of family. He would understand the families of gay and lesbian people, based on intentional choice and shared values, rather than merely on biological origin.

Jesus had some relationships that were especially deep and meaningful. From the disciples, he clearly singled out Peter, James, and John to share his most personal moments. These three men were with Jesus at pivotal times in his life and work, sharing his more private and powerful experiences. It is Peter, James, and John whom Jesus takes away with him from the crowd to pray. It is these three men who are exposed to glimpses of who Jesus really is, culminating in his transfiguration on the mountaintop in which he is seen in dazzling white robes talking with Moses and Elijah, a mystical experience the disciples don't fully comprehend. But as a result, they now see him clearly in the line of succession of Moses and the prophets. He is heir to the promises made to the Jews for their salvation.

The Gospel of John mentions one other special relationship Jesus had. To me, it is remarkable that this mention of such a relationship was left in the text. Four times, the disciple John is referred to as "the one whom Jesus loved." It is John who is depicted as reclining next to Jesus (New Revised Standard Version) and sitting on Jesus's right in the place of honor (New English Translation) at the Last Supper. The New English Translation even says, "Then the disciple whom Jesus loved leaned back against Jesus' chest" and asked him a question (John 13:25). And then, dramatically, John is depicted at the foot of the cross with Jesus's mother, watching Jesus suffer and die of crucifixion. From the cross, in moments before his death, Jesus speaks to John and his mother:

When Jesus saw his mother and the disciple whom he loved standing beside her, he said to his mother, "Woman, here is your son." Then he said to the disciple, "Here is your mother." And from that hour the disciple took her into his own home. (John 19:26–27)

Now, let me be clear. I am not saying that Jesus was gay or that he had a physically intimate relationship with "John, the Beloved Disciple," as he is known in Christian history. But one has to admit that this scene at the cross in which Jesus, in a last dying wish, asks his mother and this one disciple to treat each other as family, as mother and son, is a striking action. While it would be wrong to infer from this account more than is stated here, it would also be wrong to understate the power of what is going on here and to treat it as anything less. It would be wrong to extrapolate that Jesus and John had a physically intimate relationship, but it would also be wrong to deny that Jesus found a soul mate in this "*one* whom Jesus loved."

What can we surmise from this? It is clear to me that Jesus would not be shocked by or opposed to alternative notions of family. He would not be shocked at same-gender relationships for mutual support and productive work. He would not be surprised to see two people unrelated by blood who choose to relate to each other as if they were blood kin. He would understand the concern by one man on his deathbed for the welfare of another man, since he himself exhibited that concern.

It is clear from the record of the Gospels that Jesus had a wholly different view of women and children from his prevailing culture. Biblical Israel/Palestine was firmly patriarchal. Women and children did not count for much. In keeping with his infinite respect for all people, Jesus challenged the dominant patriarchal view that relegated women and children to second-class status. He exhibited this view in his "casual" relationships with women, freely and publicly engaging them in conversation—quite radical in his time. He did this even with foreign women, such as the "woman at the well," a much-despised-by-Jews Samaritan woman (John 4:1–30). This story even attests to the radical nature of his interchange with this woman and the disciples' reaction to it: "They were astonished that he was speaking with a woman" (John 4:27b).

As for children, Jesus exhibited a welcome unusual for a man of his time. The disciples assumed that the Master would not want to be "bothered" with children. "The disciples spoke sternly to those who brought them" (Matthew 19:13b). "But Jesus said, 'Let the little children come to me, and do not stop them; for it is to such as these that the kingdom of heaven belongs'" (Matthew 19:14). A similar account is included in Mark's Gospel, adding, "And he took them up in his arms, laid his hands on them, and blessed them" (10:13–16). The Gospel of Luke also includes this episode from Jesus's life, making it one of the few stories or sayings mentioned in all three of the Synoptic Gospels. This mention in Matthew, Mark, and Luke points not only to the surprising and remarkable nature of Jesus's attitude toward children but also to its importance in understanding his inclusion of those normally discounted by the culture.

Steeped in the Hebrew Scriptures as Jesus was, it is not surprising that he often mentions care for widows and orphans as a measure of one's compassion. While this may sound like mere kindness on Jesus's part and sympathy for someone who has lost a husband or father, it has political significance too. The reason widows and orphans were to be pitied by the culture was that they no longer had a man in their lives, and without a husband or father they had virtually no standing in society. In earlier times, and under ancient Hebrew law, the plight of a widow was so severe that a man whose brother had died was commanded to marry his brother's wife, to preserve her status in the community. Jesus's care for widows and orphans was simply another example of his reaching out to and advocating for those who had been marginalized by societal mores.

Another part of Jesus's advocacy for women related to marriage and divorce. In Jesus's time, a man could divorce a woman simply by presenting her with a writ of divorce—for any reason, or for no reason at all. She had no such right. This was indicative of the imbalance of power between a husband and a wife typical of the time. The wife's life and future were totally at the mercy of her husband. Jesus preached a radical, new equality for women in the context of marriage. He taught that the only permissible grounds for which a man might divorce his wife were unchastity. Otherwise, a man divorcing his wife was forcing his wife into adultery if she remarried. This may not seem like much progress in women's rights to the twenty-first-century mind, but it was a big step forward in Jesus's time.

What can we surmise from this? Jesus's attitude toward women and children is indicative of his commitment to the dispossessed and the marginalized. The second-class status of women and children was one of the inequities that Jesus railed against, not only with his words, but in his actions. It is impossible for me to believe that Jesus would not have a similar attitude toward homosexual people who have been treated as second-class citizens through no fault of their own. It seems entirely logical that Jesus would oppose systemic inequities and injustices for anyone.

Jesus was a rule breaker. It is clear that he was steeped in the laws of Judaism. It is at least arguable whether he ever meant to start a "church" or whether his real goal was the reformation of Judaism. It is impossible to be sure. But Jesus knew the teachings and commandments of his faith and generally believed in them. But he was not a slave to them either. On countless occasions, the scholars of Jewish law tried to catch him in not following every jot and tittle of what was prescribed. Jesus was pretty clever in getting out of these tight spots. But sometimes he openly defied the traditional teaching. When he was criticized for allowing his disciples to gather wheat on the Sabbath so they could eat (work was prohibited on that day), he proclaimed, "The Sabbath was made for humankind, not humankind for the Sabbath; so the Son of Man is lord even of the Sabbath" (Mark 2:27–28). Jesus defied the same commandment by healing the sick on the Sabbath, on a number of occasions. It seems that for him, human need trumped rules and centuries of tradition. People came first.

It seems clear that Jesus was not deterred by tradition and long-acknowledged religious thinking and custom. If people were in need and changing that thinking and tradition was required in order to respond to the needs of people, then so be it. This leads me to believe that Jesus would not shy away from equitable and humane treatment of lesbian, gay, bisexual, and transgender people, just because we have thought differently about them for centuries.

Lastly, let's look more broadly at the nature of God as revealed to the ancient Hebrews and in the person of Jesus of Nazareth. While God is often referred to as all-powerful, all-knowing, everywhere present, and Lord of all creation, there is another aspect of God that comes through more clearly and more forcefully to me: God is all-vulnerable. That may sound crazy, but let's look at the record, as told in Scripture.

In creation, God does an amazing thing. God creates humankind and gives us free will. We are free to love God back—or not. This is an astoundingly vulnerable action on God's part: to create humankind, to desire a relationship with us, indeed (if Scripture is to be believed) craving a relationship with us, and at the same time giving us the freedom to be in relationship or not. Just think of human parents, and how we desire a good, right, and loving relationship with our own children—and how vulnerable and sad we feel when it doesn't happen. So too God has made God's self vulnerable in creating us free. In doing so, God is disclosing who and what is at the center of all that is.

In Moses's call to go to Egypt to free the Israelites from the pharaoh's tyranny, Moses asks God who he should say has sent him. In the burning bush, God reveals God's name to Moses. In ancient times, knowing someone's name was powerful stuff. It enabled you to have power over someone, to give blessing and to pronounce curses. Yet God makes God's self vulnerable to God's chosen people by revealing the Holy Name and makes a covenant to love the Jews and to be their God for all time. Another act of self-disclosure and vulnerability.

For Christians, Jesus of Nazareth, who we believe is the long-awaited Messiah, is the ultimate self-revelation of God and the supreme act of vulnerability. For us, before the coming of Jesus, we were still playing a guessing game about who God was and what God was like. But in Jesus, we are told precisely just how loving God is. Rather than playing his cards close to his chest, Jesus reveals the extravagant and ready-to-forgive love God has for us. No more guessing. When the Prodigal Son returns from a life of riotous living, ready to confess his sin to his father and work as a slave in his fields, he is met by his father while still on the road, where his father isn't interested in his prepared apology, but rather only cares that the boy has returned home. Instead of stern words, the father offers a ring for his finger, a new robe, and a "welcome home" party. That, Jesus tells his disciples, is what God's attitude is toward humankind.

It seems to me, then, that vulnerability and self-disclosure are at the heart of what we understand about the nature of God. And the reason I believe gay and lesbian people are spiritual people is that we too have participated in vulnerability and self-disclosure, especially in the process of coming-out. When someone shares with you who they really, really are, it is a special offering. To do so when it risks rejection is a profound, holy gift.

Someone who comes out as gay puts himself in a very vulnerable position, not knowing how that new knowledge will affect relationships. It may destroy a friendship. It may cause a parent to throw her own child out onto the streets. It may cause a child to reject her gay dad. But it is an act of self-disclosure that makes true relationship possible. This kind of vulnerability and self-disclosure I would label "of God." That is, it participates in the very deepest understanding of what we know about God.

No one can ever know the mind of God completely. No one can say for sure what Jesus would think and do in response to a twenty-first-century development. But for me, it is hard to imagine that Jesus wouldn't take a kindly, supportive attitude toward the love felt for each other by two people of the same gender. Can anyone imagine that Jesus would denounce and decry two men or two women who have fallen in love, have promised to live in a faithful, monogamous, lifelong-intentioned relationship, and now seek the civil status and the Church's sacrament of marriage? I cannot.

At the very least, surely we can agree that it would be completely within the bounds of what we have come to expect from Jesus that he would reach out to those discriminated against and pushed to the margins by a hostile society. Surely he would speak out against antigay violence and advocate respect for all of God's children, including God's lesbian, gay, bisexual, and transgender children. Surely he would support stable, enduring, and loving relationships for the raising of children. Surely he would see the promises pledged in marriage by one man to another man, by one woman to another woman, as life-giving and holy. It would be totally out of character for Jesus to do anything else.

CHAPTER 6

Doesn't Gay Marriage Change the Definition of Marriage That's Been in Place for Thousands of Years?

No Episcopal priest is allowed to solemnize and bless a marriage unless premarital counseling has been done by the officiant or another priest of the church. It is a statement about the seriousness with which the Church goes about marriage.

Each priest decides what the nature and content of that marriage preparation will be. At the end of the first session, where I ask the couple to tell me the story of their meeting, falling in love, and then wanting to make the commitment of marriage to each other, I give them a survey of questions about all aspects of their relationship. They are asked not to answer the questions but to indicate that

(a) this is something we are in agreement about, (b) this is something we are in some disagreement about, or (c) this is not something we've really discussed.

What is most revealing about this questionnaire is the way it uncovers different levels of trust, commitment, and understanding between the two. One partner is convinced that a particular topic has been fully discussed and agreed upon, while the other is not at all sure. At least some gaps in communication are readily revealed. These gaps give me the opportunity to invite better communication between the two parties. Sometimes the presence of a third—and trustworthy—person gives one of the partners the courage to bring up a disparity that is too frightening to risk raising, now that the wedding invitations have been sent out.

Not a single issue raised in these several sessions of premarital counseling is specific to or exclusively relevant to opposite-gender marriage. Which has led me to wonder if same-gender marriage changes the definition of marriage at all!

You are not alone in wondering if we aren't tampering with a time-honored, hallowed tradition and practice. It feels a little like defying the gods! But I know it's not unusual for people to think that what they have experienced in their own lives is the way it has always been. The facts about the history and evolution of marriage show that that is not the case.

Some people would have you believe that marriage

began with Adam and Eve. But in the account in Genesis where Adam and Eve become one flesh (presumably through their mutual commitment and sexual intimacy), there is no mention of an "institution" of marriage nor any liturgy, vows, promises, or other ritual used to solemnize their relationship. This prehistorical account can only serve as a backdrop to the meaning (not the "institution") of marriage that developed over time.

The fact of the matter is, marriage has *not* been consistent or unchanging over time. Indeed, even in biblical times, we see a constant evolution in the practice of marriage. One man and one woman, united in marriage for life, mutually exclusive and "faithful" sexually, and joined because of their love for each other, is a relatively modern notion of marriage. Such was not the case in ancient times.

Marriage in Old Testament Times

From the earliest Old Testament accounts, polygamy seemed to be the practice of the day. Or, to be more accurate, polygyny (the practice of polygamy by males, not females) was practiced. In the ancient Hebrew culture, having more than one wife was commonplace. In addition to multiple wives, men who were wealthy enough to have slaves or concubines had sexual relationships with them. Even Abraham—father to Judaism, Islam, and

Christianity—when he was unable to produce an heir with his wife, Sarah, had a son by his slave Hagar. Abraham's grandson Jacob married two sisters, Leah and Rachel. King Solomon was renowned not only for his wisdom and wealth but also for his seven hundred wives and three hundred concubines! Over the years, marriage customs evolved, and by Jesus's time divorce was discouraged and monogamy increasingly became the standard.

Ancient Israel was fiercely patriarchal, and for the purposes of marriage women had no rights. Divorce was permitted by a husband for some "uncleanness" in his wife, and that divorce was accomplished simply by giving her a "bill of divorce" and sending her away. Women had no rights in this regard and under most circumstances could not divorce their husbands.

In parts of the Old Testament, and at various times in Israel's history, a man was required to marry his brother's wife if the brother's death left his widow childless. To be a female, or a child, without a man in the house as husband or father was thought to be a terrible thing—which is why so much attention is paid to widows and orphans by Israel's prophets, and later by Jesus.

Marital arrangements were negotiated by the husband-to-be and the bride's father and carried all the traits of an economic transaction. Affection or love might be present, or might develop over the years, but was certainly not a prerequisite of marriage.

Teachings on Marriage and Divorce
by Jesus and Saint Paul

Jesus was quite radical in his regard for women. Not only did they follow him as disciples, but they are said to have funded his ministry financially. He resisted many of the teachings and proscriptions about women from his Scriptures (the Hebrew Scriptures), for which he was roundly criticized.

Jesus is quite clear that marriage is to be for a lifetime and that divorce is a serious issue, permitted to a man only in the case of "unchastity." For either a man or a woman to marry anyone after divorce ("except on the ground of unchastity"), Jesus tells his disciples, is to commit "adultery" (Matthew 19: 9; 5:31–32; Mark 10:11–12; Luke 16:18). Jesus does seem to imply that divorce because of unchastity is allowable for women as well as men, representing more marital rights for women than had been previously taught.

Saint Paul can hardly be said to be supportive of marriage. The early Church expected the imminent return of Jesus in the Second Coming, and life was to be lived as purely and purposefully as possible until that event. Paul gives a nod to human reality and passion by begrudgingly offering a concession for the meantime: "To the unmarried and the widows I say that it is well for them to remain unmarried as I am. But if they are not practicing self-control, they should marry. For it is better to marry than to be aflame with passion" (1 Corinthians 7:8–9).

Paul does promote a kind of egalitarianism in marriage, balancing the husband's authority over his wife and her body with an equal authority for the wife over the husband and his body (1 Corinthians 7:4). It is not at all certain, and highly questionable, that such egalitarianism in marriage was practiced in such a patriarchal society.

Holy Scripture and "Family Values"

While looking at the institution of marriage as practiced and taught in the New Testament, we must be very careful not to project our current understanding of marriage and "family values" back onto an ancient time, when such notions would have been foreign to that culture. It must be noted that the model of family we have today—that is, the so-called nuclear family—would have been unknown in ancient times, when the extended family was the norm. Married couples often lived in a household with parents, children, and other relatives. People were much less mobile than today, and families lived, worked, and socialized as extended family units. One man married to one woman, living in a home with only their children, was a rarity.

The teachings of Jesus can hardly be used to support the notion of the modern nuclear family—or even the idea of the biological family. Jesus had some things to say about families and familial relationships that sound harsh to modern ears. Indeed, he seemed to promote a family based *not* on biological origin but on intention, choice, and shared beliefs.

Matthew's Gospel records an incident in which Jesus is speaking publicly, when he is told that his "mother and brothers are standing outside, wanting to speak to [him]. But to the one who had told him this, Jesus replied, 'Who is my mother, and who are my brothers?' And pointing to his disciples, he said, 'Here are my mother and my brothers! For whoever does the will of my Father in heaven is my brother and sister and mother'" (Matthew 12:46–50).

Jesus's closest companions were a dozen men who followed his call to become his disciples. It is also clear that Jesus had other disciples beyond "the twelve," including women. In addition, Jesus singled out three of the disciples (Peter, James, and John) whom he groomed for leadership.

Even so, in addition to these three disciples, there was "the one whom Jesus loved." John, the so-called Beloved Disciple, is identified this way only in the Gospel of John and may have been his followers' way of giving their mentor special status among the disciples. But still, it is remarkable that one of the official accounts of Jesus's life, authorized by the early Church to be a canonical book of Scripture, would name a particular person as "the one whom Jesus loved" (John 13:23). It is this same disciple who is identified as standing next to Jesus's mother, Mary, at the cross, witnessing Jesus's crucifixion. Seeing them, Jesus says, from the cross, to his mother, " 'Woman, here is your son.' Then he said to the disciple, 'Here is your mother.' And from that hour the disciple took her into his own home" (John 19:26–27).

Now, I am *not* saying Jesus was gay or that he had any sort of sexual intimacy with "John, the Beloved Disciple" or anyone else! Still, it is remarkable that one disciple was singled out as "the one" whom Jesus loved, the same one pictured as reclining beside Jesus at the Last Supper, and the same one to whom Jesus spoke from the cross, telling him to take Mary as his own mother, and for Mary to take John as her son. I am not saying or even implying more than the text itself states, but I *am* cautioning us not to put into Jesus's mouth or mind modern notions of marriage and the nuclear family. According to the Scriptures themselves, Jesus seems to have gathered around him an intentionally chosen group of people whom he regarded as his family (and one especially)—more deeply so than his own biological family.

Marriage in the Early and Medieval Centuries

For many centuries, marriage continued to be a civil and private matter. Over the years, Christianity began to have an influence over the institution of marriage, "Christianizing" some of the harsher variations of it found in Western Europe. Germanic marriage custom offered an almost purely economic understanding of marriage, seeing it as a business deal between father and husband, who agreed on a mutually acceptable "bride price," payable in full when the bride was delivered to the husband at the wedding. (About all the bride got out of this tidy arrangement was a wedding ring—signifying that an agreeable price had been reached between her father and her husband-to-be. Later, other more ethereal and symbolic meanings would be attached to this ring, but originally it was no more than a symbolic down payment on the agreed-upon bride price.)

Eventually, the Church began to exercise more influence over the practice of and conditions for marriage, articulating various impediments to it, including prohibitions against marriage to those deemed "too close" by blood. The Church became involved in investigations of these impediments, declaring an annulment for those found to be in violation of these impediments (necessary, since divorce was increasingly forbidden). Even so, the Church still regarded marriage as a civil and private matter. Not until the twelfth century did a priest of the Church become involved in wedding rites, and not until the thirteenth century did the priest actually take charge of the service.

Consistent throughout this time, the consent of those being married was essential, although given the disparity between the rights of men and those of women, and the economic dependence of one on the other, it is hard to imagine that the woman's consent was as genuine or real as that of her husband-to-be or her father. In the case of marriages arranged for children (for economic or sociopolitical reasons), the modern mind would not understand the "consent" given (cajoled or coerced) by these children to be in any way "meaningful" consent.

Marriage After the Reformation

Along with all the other changes brought by the Reformation, marriage became, according to Martin Luther, "a worldly thing . . . that belongs to the realm of government." English Puritans believed marriage to be purely secular, and although religious oversight of marriage was restored when the Puritans lost power in England, the Puritans brought this secular understanding of marriage with them to America, where it persisted.

In response to the Reformation, the Roman Catholic Church reasserted and strengthened its authority over marriages, now requiring that the marriage be presided over by a priest and witnessed by two other people. This ended secret marriages as well as those marriages that were never formally solemnized, but rather were simply deemed to be marriages by virtue of the couple's mutual consent and common domicile. These came to be known as common-law marriages and continued to be recognized in some states in America until 1970.

In most of Western Europe, marriage became a civil matter and remains so to this day. Those who wish a religious community's blessing on a marriage may obtain it only after a civil ceremony presided over by the State.

Interracial Marriage

Generally speaking, most modern cultures have prohibited marriage between people of two races, most notably in America (during and after slavery), in Nazi Germany, and during the years of apartheid in South Africa.

Slaves in America did marry, but such marriages were not legally recognized. The slave owner could still buy and sell "married" slaves, often separating husband from wife and destroying families in the process. Oddly enough, some slave owners encouraged marriage among their slaves— partly to assuage criticism by abolitionists and partly to render their slaves more reluctant to run away. Marriage, recognized by the State, was one of the more sought after of newfound rights that came with freedom, and by the early twentieth century most African-Americans were legally married.

What continued not to be recognized and affirmed was marriage between the races. Miscegenation (a combination of the Latin words *miscere,* "to mix," and *genus,* or "kind") was strictly forbidden, and antimiscegenation laws were common across the United States. Several attempts (from 1871 to 1928) were made to write antimiscegenation laws into the U.S. Constitution, though these efforts failed. State antimiscegenation laws continued in many places until 1967, when the U.S. Supreme Court declared such laws unconstitutional (*Loving v. Virginia*), thereby striking down those laws in the sixteen states that still had them. President Barack Obama's parents could not have been married in these sixteen states prior to 1967.

The right to marry was a hard-fought civil right in the United States long after the end of the Civil War. Yet this was a fight not over the *meaning* of marriage but over who was *eligible* to participate in this institution. African-Americans as well as couples of two different races were not arguing over the importance or meaning of marriage but rather fighting for their civil right to participate in this noble institution. They were not trying to redefine the meaning of marriage but only attempting to become eligible for its traditional meaning and practice. The definition of marriage was not changed by the opening of access to it for African-Americans.

I would argue that such is the case with our current debates over marriage for same-gender couples. At the end of the day, this is a very conservative argument being made for gay marriage. After all, gay and lesbian couples are seeking not to destroy the institution of marriage but to join it! Gay couples want out of marriage what heterosexual couples want—respect, recognition, protections (even from a spouse in the case of divorce), a wholesome environment in which to raise children, and legal rights and financial benefits by which government rewards and supports the stability of society that marriage promotes.

As we can see, the understanding of marriage has not been constant throughout history, but rather has been gradually evolving over time. Surely none of us would agree with or condone marriage practices in biblical times (either Old or New Testament). Few of us would hope for or espouse the inequality of men and women so typified by marriage arrangements of the past. Indeed, as a clergyman and representative of the State in marriage, I have tried my best (as have many others) to deprive the rite of marriage of its sexist, women-as-property ingredients. The father "giving" his daughter in marriage to the husband has been replaced with both mother and father "presenting" their daughter to the groom and both mother and father of the groom "presenting" their son to the bride. Though initially surprised and sometimes shocked by such proposals for changes in marriage traditions, the bride and groom and their families have generally (and enthusiastically) embraced such changes as better expressions of what they actually feel and intend.

We all now agree that freely offered, mutual, and romantic love is an essential ingredient in a marriage. Such romantic feelings of love have not been considered a prerequisite of marriage for most of history, and mutual love was only a happenstance by-product of such a union, not its purpose. Our understanding and practice of marriage have been in constant change over the centuries, bringing us to a common understanding of marriage as a mutual commitment, entered into freely and by mutual consent, by two people who love each other, pledge their fidelity and trustworthiness to each other, and wish their union to be a blessing both to any children that come from it and to the society as a whole. In doing so, they intend to contribute to the stability of society. In return, they expect from society the respect and social recognition of their commitment to each other and its attendant benefits.

Gay and lesbian couples in general want exactly that. Nothing more. But also nothing less. Proponents of marriage for gay or lesbian couples are not changing or undermining the *meaning* or *definition* of marriage; rather, they are merely seeking the right for gay or lesbian couples to be *eligible* for its responsibilities and benefits, both legal and social. Marriage for gay or lesbian couples is not an undoing of the meaning and purpose of marriage but rather its natural and appropriate evolution.

CHAPTER 7

Doesn't Gay Marriage
Undermine Marriage?

The morning after passage of the marriage equality bill in New York, I got a call from a friend and his partner, asking if I would preside at their marriage, now scheduled for the fall. I called the priest at a church I know in New York, to see if we might be able to hold the service there.

Episcopal priests are required to do premarital counseling with all those who desire to be married and have their marriage blessed by the Church. This is the last thing on the minds of many heterosexual couples who seek to be married. Indeed, a priest is usually contacted long after a couple makes a decision to be married, and well after a caterer, florist, and reception venue have been secured.

This priest remarked about how willing and eager gay and lesbian couples are to do the premarital counseling. "They take the sacrament of marriage so much more seriously, and go about it with so much more intentionality, than heterosexual couples," he told me. That is true of my experience as well. Instead of seeing this counseling as something to be endured rather than embraced, gay and lesbian couples seem to relish the opportunity to explore the meaning of marriage, the factors that contribute to or detract from a good relationship, and the spiritual foundations of a good marriage. This seems to be true whether the couple has been together only for a year or two or for twenty, thirty, or forty years.

Perhaps it is because legal marriage between two men or two women is a new thing. Perhaps it is because the right to marry has been denied for so long that when it finally comes, they want to take advantage of every opportunity to deepen their relationship as they enter this new chapter in their lives. And perhaps, as gay marriage becomes as commonplace and uncontroversial as heterosexual marriage, it too will be taken for granted. But for now, gay couples are being extraordinarily thoughtful and intentional about this decision to marry. At a time when more and more heterosexual couples are choosing to live together, even make a life together, without the benefit of marriage, it is gay and lesbian couples who are holding up and affirming the traditional values associated with marriage.

As I ended my conversation with this priest, I said to

him, "Wouldn't it be ironic if instead of undermining marriage, as it often is alleged, gay marriage was its salvation?!"

One of the arguments made against the right to marry for gay or lesbian couples is that such a move would undermine the institution of marriage. Marriage is under assault from so many sides, do we really need to experiment with this much-beleaguered institution?

There is no question that the institution of marriage has seen better days, at least if you judge by the declining percentage of people choosing to live in wedlock. Marriage used to be the norm for most heterosexual couples, especially for those who desired a family and children. Intercourse outside the state of marriage was condemned by the church and the synagogue, and a child conceived and raised out of wedlock was both frowned upon and rare, except perhaps among the poor. Pregnant girls were whisked away under cover of darkness to homes especially set up for their care. Adoptions were arranged, and the girls would return home amid whispers of scandal and a tarnished reputation. Many of these young men and women and their parents would hastily arrange a "shotgun wedding," to provide legitimacy (retrospectively, of course) for the child and a somewhat diminished respectability for the couple.

With the advent of the women's movement in the 1970s, questions were increasingly raised about the inherent power differential in most marriages, based on gender.

Women began asking questions about why such a difference in power between the genders had to exist. "Because that's the way it's always been" ceased to be a good enough reason to participate in a patriarchal arrangement that had been the tradition for countless millennia.

Many women began to question the institution of marriage itself, wondering aloud if such an institution could be transformed and adapted or whether the entire institution needed to be discarded. Some women chose to forgo marriage itself, opting instead to live with a male partner but not marry him. Unmarried women who became pregnant were not as ready to marry for the sake of reputation, understanding that such marriages had a poor chance of survival. Even parents began to question whether making their seventeen-year-old daughter marry the eighteen-year-old father of her baby was in the long-term interest of her, the boy, or their baby.

Note that these changes in attitudes toward the institution of marriage predate any discussion of gay marriage, never mind its legalization. Alongside the decline in attitudes toward marriage was an increase in the respectability of single life. Where it was once assumed that all people *wanted* to be married, whether or not they were ever successful in finding a marriage partner, society began to regard the single life as an honorable choice. The single life *with children* became more common and more acceptable in society, though most single parents had been previously married and produced offspring within the institution of marriage. Still, growing numbers of single people chose to have a family through alternative means (adoption, artificial insemination, and so on) without the benefit of marriage. And for the first time, at the beginning of this century, married couples became a minority in the United States. Indeed, the 2006 report of the American Community Survey showed that 50.3 percent of American households were headed by unmarried people. Married-couple households were now a minority at 49.7 percent.

Not only is there less pressure to *get* married, but there is more stress on those who *are* married, often ending in divorce. By every measurement available, the greatest stressor on marriages is money and the problems associated with it. Damon Carr, in the article "Until 'Debt' Do Us Part," wrote on November 24, 2003, that nearly 80 percent of divorced or divorcing couples cite financial problems as the leading cause of their marriage's demise.

The threat of economic hardship, or poverty itself, can generate tremendous stress on a marriage. In the so-called Great Recession starting in 2008, married couples saw their greatest assets, their homes, shrink in value to below what was owed on their mortgages. Being "underwater" severely diminishes a married couple's options. If the husband's or wife's job requires a move, can the couple afford to do so without taking a crippling loss on their house? They may not be able to sell at all, given the glut of properties on the market. In an "underwater" situation, there is no equity to be utilized when economic hardship threatens. With the loss of a job, by one or both of the married partners, the financial stress can lead to foreclosure on the home. This loss of financial viability and the diminishment of options available to the couple put the marriage in a veritable state of siege, from which many couples never recover and which for many results in divorce.

Add to the financial pressure on marriages in the twenty-first century these other stressors, most often listed by married couples as reasons for their divorce: abuse (emotional and physical), addictions (alcohol being a huge component in many marital difficulties), adultery, "bed death" (the loss of physical intimacy between the couple), and the inability and/or unwillingness to deal with conflict.

Marriage is hard work. If one or both partners are unwilling or unable to do their share of the work on the relationship, the chances of the marriage falling apart are great. If it doesn't end in divorce, it still may cause pain and disappointment to everyone touched by it. Even in the best of circumstances, people change over time. All of us grow and develop. A couple may marry at twenty or thirty years old and find themselves quite different people at forty or fifty. If one or both of the spouses are unwilling to work hard to keep their marriage vows current, as both people change over time, the likelihood of the marriage surviving is greatly reduced.

When these stressors present themselves, one or both partners in the marriage may not have the communication skills to engage in honest discussions about disagreements. One partner often shares feelings openly and readily, while the other is loath to do so. Some couples make the decision to have another child as a way of bringing them closer—a terrible reason to bring a child into the world and one that seldom improves the relationship between husband and wife. If that marriage ends in divorce, it just means one more human being is affected by the failed marriage.

The point of rehearsing all these stressors on marriage in a book on gay marriage is to say that yes, the institution of marriage is under great stress. Many conditions and circumstances are undermining it. But nothing in all the data suggests that the existence of legal marriages between people of the same gender affects marriages between heterosexual men and women. As the brief discussion above summarizes, there are plenty of reasons for marriages to be unhappy and stressful and end in divorce. But none of them relate to the existence of gay marriage.

Opponents of gay marriage who claim they are worried about undermining the institution of marriage might instead spend their time and money on equipping couples with communication skills, helping them explore their values and practices around money, and providing them with tools for dealing with conflict. They might devote themselves to job creation in an economy that is pushing more and more people into poverty every day, putting enormous stress on marriages. Blaming gay marriage for the demise of the institution of marriage is simply a red herring from people who seem to have no interest at all in doing anything about the actual conditions that cause marriages to fail.

There is, on the other hand, one circumstance in which gay marriage and heterosexual marriage directly affect each other. Many gay men and lesbians, who grew up prior to open discussions about and increasing acceptance of homosexuality, married opposite-gender partners. For most, this was not a brazen attempt at disguising themselves or providing "cover" for their closeted sexuality. Many gay men and lesbians truly wanted a family and children. Pretending to be someone they were not was the cost of admission to the institution of marriage and the family they desired.

That pretending often came with a terrible price. Gay husbands or lesbian wives often experienced a painful disconnect and alienation from their true selves. Some dealt with that pain by becoming addicted to alcohol, drugs, or work. Some became distant from their spouses, physically and emotionally. Sometimes there were furtive affairs, followed by guilt and despair. And then, for many, the pain became too great to bear, and they came out to their spouses and sought a way forward that was honest and full of integrity. For some, that meant staying married with renegotiated understandings of expectations and vows. For most, it meant divorce—sometimes amicable and supportive of each other, acknowledging the love each still held for the other, and sometimes vicious and angry, with horrifying child custody battles and efforts to destroy any future life for the offending party.

It is true that the catalyst for such a coming-out is, sometimes, falling in love with someone of the same gender while being heterosexually married. Many married gay men and lesbians know they are gay but find the courage to leave a marriage only when they meet someone with whom they experience the deep and profound joy that comes from expressing their true selves. Often they want to spend their lives with this person, and divorce becomes an option for the first time. In this way only can it be said that gay marriage affects the institution of marriage.

But in fact, such a situation argues *for* gay marriage, not against it. In a world that is more accepting of gay and lesbian people, there is less need to hide who one is. There is less pressure to appear "straight." Certainly, with the existence of gay marriage, there is no reason to have to get married to someone of the opposite sex just to have a family. The more examples of wholesome, happy, and thriving gay marriages we have, the less frequently we will have heterosexual marriages destroyed when one of the partners discovers his or her sexual orientation, comes out, and leaves the marriage. These marriages will diminish as it becomes more and more acceptable to be gay or lesbian. Gay marriage, and the acceptability it signals, will save many people from a marriage that will end in divorce.

The legal option for same-gender partners to get married would actually reduce the pressure to enter into a dishonest relationship with someone of the opposite gender. Gay marriage would largely eliminate the one particular set of circumstances that, it could be argued, undermine some marriages.

Quite contrary to the notion that gay marriage undermines the institution of marriage, gay and lesbian couples seem to be making the loudest and deepest arguments for the institution of marriage. While heterosexual couples are choosing to live together without the benefit of marriage in increasing numbers, gay and lesbian couples are marching in the streets and voting at the ballot box for the right to be married. Even heterosexual married couples sometimes wonder why this is so important to gay or lesbian couples. One of my favorite cartoons shows a couple, obviously married for a long time, with the husband saying, "Gay people getting married??!! Haven't they suffered enough?!"

If marriage is being undermined, it is being done by those heterosexual couples who see no need to go through the formality of a state or church wedding. Besides, if things don't work out, it's easier to get out of such an informal arrangement. If proponents of the sanctity of marriage are looking for allies, they might best look to homosexuals.

Gay and lesbian couples are extremely intentional in the words and practices associated with their weddings. More than most straight couples (in my experience, and reflective of the experience of clergy I know), gay couples want every word of their liturgy to have integrity, to be true for them, to speak truthfully about who they are and who they hope to be individually and as a couple.

Heterosexual couples tend to think about the religious service of marriage *after* they've decided on a date, a reception venue, a caterer, a florist, and a honeymoon destination. The service to be used and the words to be said are sometimes almost afterthoughts. In contrast, a gay or lesbian couple is more apt to begin the marriage process by finding someone to preside at a service, inquiring as to what words might be used in a liturgy, and asking if certain ideas they have about their service might be incorporated. This is delightfully refreshing for clergy, who are, more often than not, consulted with less solemnity than the caterer.

Straight couples will often inquire, "Do we have to use the word 'God' in our ceremony?" This leads many of us clergy to wonder if our churches are being used as beautiful backdrops for the wedding photographs rather than as spiritual centers in which God's blessing is to be pronounced on the marriage. Gay couples, on the other hand, almost never ask for God to be absented in any way. They desire God's blessing on them and their marriage. Gay couples are more likely to want a very traditional wedding, using familiar and traditional words, vows, and actions. After all, this is the institution from which they have been barred for so long, and now that it's here, they want to embrace that institution for which they have fought. If they desire language different from the traditional service, it is usually in an effort to strip the liturgy of its patriarchal vestiges and to make it a service that the couple can participate in without reservation.

This is also part of the gay community's insistence upon the word "marriage." We have worked in our relationships for the depth of commitment evident in traditional marriage. We have sought our equal rights for access to this social institution. We want our families to have the recognized and affirmed respect that other families have, by virtue of their being "married." And that's why the word is so important to us.

Far from undermining marriage, gay and lesbian couples seeking marriage for themselves are perhaps the institution's best friends. At a time when marriage is seen as less desirable and less necessary for straight couples, gay and lesbian people are lining up at town halls and church doors to participate in this traditional and long-standing institution.

Gay marriage not only doesn't undermine the institution of marriage; it actually lends credence and support to marriage at a time when it is threatened and undermined by a wide range of circumstances. Champions of marriage should be delighted at the prospect of gay men and lesbians seeking to join in the tradition and practice of marriage.

CHAPTER 8

What If My Religion Doesn't Believe in Gay Marriage?

Separation of Church and State is a beloved foundation of the freedoms enjoyed in the United States of America. Yet, oddly, it is found more profoundly in other places—France, Uruguay, Scandinavia, and, until recently, even Turkey. In America, while we claim a separation of Church and State, the practice is much more confusing.

Virtually no one running for office can do so as an atheist. Such a self-proclamation would sound the death knell for any candidate. Those trying to court the vote of the religious Right often pepper their public statements with code words and phrases that indicate an evangelical bent. Candidates of both major parties are scrutinized for how big a role their religious values would play in their decision making. Nominees for the Supreme Court are often quizzed about their religious background, in an effort to determine how they might rule on a particular case. While we claim that Church (which in this context includes the synagogue, mosque, and any other religious institution) and State are separated in this country, the fact of the matter is that religion plays a substantial role in our thinking and our public life.

There can be no question that religion has played a huge role in the search for equal civil rights for lesbian, gay, bisexual, and transgender people. Opposition to equal rights for this particular minority comes principally from a religious understanding that homosexuality is simply wrong. Even those who are not practicing religionists themselves are affected by the religious opposition to homosexuality "in the air" of a significantly Judeo-Christian culture.

Teasing Church and State apart is difficult and dangerous work. Those attempting to do so are open to accusations of being antireligion. While we know that America is living in a post-Christian era, one might never suspect it, given the nature of the public debate over marriage equality.

Is marriage a religious institution or a civil institution? The answer is it is both. And therein lies the confusion and controversy for gay marriage.

The First Amendment to the Constitution begins with the words "Congress shall make no law respecting an establishment of religion, or prohibiting the free exercise thereof." That is, the State will not pass laws that establish a state religion, nor will the State prefer one religion over another, a religion over non-religion, nor conversely non-religion over religion. This so-called establishment and free exercise clause in the First Amendment has been much debated, particularly in the latter half of the twentieth century. Still, in America, it is the foundational bedrock for the free practice of religion without interference from the government.

Known as the separation of Church and State, it is more accurately described as the separation of Religion and State, since other religious communities outside and beyond Christendom are protected from state interference as well. Not until late in the twentieth century was this clause interpreted by the U.S. Supreme Court as applying not just to laws enacted by Congress but also to state and local municipalities.

In the current debate over marriage equality, many religious organizations argue that laws permitting marriage between two people of the same gender violate their protections against the government meddling in their internal affairs, that is, their definition of marriage. This needs to be sorted out in order to make a fair assessment of whether gay marriage violates this long-held civil value.

This issue has gotten very confused, in part because both the Church ("Church" is meant to include all religious bodies seeking protection under the establishment clause) and the State use the same word—"marriage"—for the joining of two people. But do they each mean the same thing when that word is used?

For the Church, marriage is the joining of one man and one woman in holy matrimony. In some denominations, marriage is considered one of the sacraments (albeit one of the "lesser" sacraments, like confirmation or ordination). As we have seen, however, the Church (at least the Christian Church) came to the "marrying business" somewhat late, that is in the Middle Ages, as a sacrament to be entered into by all church members seeking such a social arrangement. Before that time, marriage was strictly a civil matter. Still, in the minds of most Americans, marriage is something that is done in churches and other places of worship. And so, if the government is going to prescribe who can and cannot be married, it would seem that the State is interfering with the internal workings of religious groups, prohibited under the establishment and free exercise clause in the First Amendment.

But let's actually examine what takes place, say in that sweet little church out in the country (so perfect for a wedding!), St. Swithin's-by-the-Gas-Pump. What is actually going on at such a wedding? What makes the couple married? How is the State involved? How is the Church involved? Who's in charge here?

Forget all the flower arrangements, bridesmaids' dresses, and little bags of rice (or the more ecological birdseed) to be thrown over the departing couple. Let's focus instead on what is happening, legally and theologically.

The simple fact of the matter is that regardless of what happens at the church service, regardless of what vows are mutually undertaken by the bride and groom, regardless of whether there are wedding rings exchanged and worn, what makes the couple married in the eyes of the State is the marriage license completed by the bride and groom *and then signed by an authorized agent of the State!* In truth, it is that signature by a representative of the State that makes a couple married. That signature witnesses to the agreement by the couple, stated or unstated in a formal service, to seek the legal status of marriage with each other, freely and without coercion, and to obtain the State's legal recognition of that status. Proof of age has been required in order to get the marriage license, to conform to state laws. The couple becomes married when an authorized representative of the State completes that marriage license by signing it and returning it to the Town Clerk or other administrative body.

The State does not care what words are used at the religious ceremony, nor does it care about the content of any vows exchanged. The State does not confer any blessing on the union, other than the benefits that come from the legal recognition of marital status—tax benefits, inheritance rights, and a host of other state and federal benefits. The State doesn't care whether the person signing the marriage certificate, thereby enacting the marriage, is an ordained person or a justice of the peace. In fact, in many states, absolutely anyone can obtain from the state's Office of the Secretary of State a one-day license to officiate at a wedding. No credentials are required. That person, whoever he or she may be, is deputized for that day to act as a representative of the State. When he or she signs the marriage license and returns it to the Town Clerk, the couple is married in the eyes of the State.

The marriage issue has become so confused in this country because, for a very long time now, the State has automatically deputized ordained clergy to act as agents of the State in officiating at weddings. The rules and requirements may vary slightly from state to state, but generally any ordained person residing in the State is officially sanctioned to represent the state in authorizing a marriage. Clergy from outside the state are often required to receive the same one-day authorization from the secretary of state that non-clergy must apply for, but usually there is no question raised about any clergyperson performing this function for the State.

All of the above functioning generally takes place beyond the view of those attending the wedding. Usually, no one sees the marriage license, no one witnesses the signing of the marriage license (except the Town Clerk who guides the couple through its completion), and no one sees the officiant or clergyperson sign and return it to the Town Clerk's office. No wonder that attendees at the wedding ceremony assume it is the service itself, and the clergy's pronouncement that the man and woman "are now husband and wife," that make the couple married.

Even the Church—at least in its theological thinking—

acknowledges that the clergyperson is not the one "administering the sacrament" of marriage. That is, for a very long time, the Church has understood that it is not the clergyperson who marries the couple but rather the bride and groom who marry *each other.* It is the bride and groom who act as agents of this sacramental act.

So what is the clergyperson there to do? Primarily, the clergy are present to ask, on behalf of the community, God's blessing on the union just created by the bride and groom. It is the Church's (or other religious body's) blessing that the couple seeks by marrying each other in the presence of a worshipping community. Also, most religions understand that the gathered community of family and friends who have come to witness and celebrate the marriage add their own "blessing" to that offered by the Church. In some liturgies, the assembled congregation is asked, "Will those of you who witness these vows do all in your power to support and uphold them in their marriage?" The congregation responds with a hearty "We do!"

In simple shorthand, the State marries and the Church blesses.

It is also commonly understood that those who are married "without benefit of clergy" are indeed married in the eyes of the State and in the eyes of most of its citizens. When someone tells you he or she is married, most people would not follow up with the question of whether that marriage was accomplished in a religious setting or "merely" by a justice of the peace. Those married by a civil magistrate (even a "magistrate for a day") are considered just as married as those who have a big church wedding.

Indeed in many countries—France, for instance—everyone is married at the mayor's office. This constitutes full and complete marriage. Then those who are religious gather with family and friends at their place of worship for whatever that religious tradition does to bless that marriage. This makes the separation between what the State does (marry) and what the religious community does (bless). Again, because in America both of these functions are generally done in the same place, led by the same people, they have become blurred in their meaning. When guests attend a religious wedding, few know where the civil part of the ceremony begins and ends and where the religious ceremony takes over. Probably, most people never even consider this distinction. We are simply on autopilot in our thinking. Gay marriage calls for a clearer delineation.

So how can we educate the electorate about this rightful separation of Church and State? I am attempting, in my own Episcopal Diocese of New Hampshire, to untangle the mess and confusion we've gotten ourselves into. I have been encouraging my clergy to "get out of the marriage business." That is, I believe we could make great progress if clergy stopped acting as agents of the State in the civil administration of marriages.

Let's return to that beloved little church, St. Swithin's, for a look at how such a separation might occur for the benefit of all. A couple—gay or straight—comes to the priest announcing their desire to be married at St. Swithin's next June. The priest responds, "Congratulations! I am so happy for you. Now, let me tell you how we do weddings at St. Swithin's. You probably know Sam Marriagemaker, the senior warden and chair of our vestry here at St. Swithin's. He's the person we have asked to act as an agent of the State in officiating at all marriages. At the beginning of the service, all your family and friends will gather around you and Sam for the marriage. We'll do this at the back of the church, symbolically at the door where the secular and the sacred meet. Sam will do the secular, civil part of the service—the legal marriage itself. He will sign the marriage license and return it to the Town Clerk.

"After Sam has accomplished the marriage and pronounced you married, we'll invite your guests to return to the pews of the church, and we'll sing a beautiful hymn as you both process up the aisle as a married couple. Then I, acting as the priest and president of this religious community, will take over and do what the Church does: bless. We'll have Scripture readings, a brief homily, and then a restatement of your vows, this time asking God to be a part of your marriage, asking God's help in living up to those vows. We will also ask your family and friends gathered if they will support you in this holy endeavor and hold you accountable for the promises you have made to each other. And then, acting on behalf of God, the Church, and those gathered, I will pray a blessing over you as a couple, asking God to richly bless your lives as you seek to fulfill the vows you have made."

Think of how clear and "clean" this action would be.

Think of how clarifying—for everyone present—this would be, embodying the separation between what the State does and what the Church does.

The prospect of divorce also clarifies what is going on and who is in charge. When a marriage ends in divorce, the once-loving couple does not return to the sweet, little St. Swithin's-by-the-Gas-Pump to obtain their divorce. They go to the courts! They understand, if they haven't already, that the State presides over the institution of marriage, not religious bodies. (One exception to this is in Judaism, where couples sign a marriage contract, or *ketubah,* and must return to an Orthodox rabbi/court to secure a *get* in which the original contract is broken.)

Now that we understand the difference between what the religious body does and what the State does in the process of marrying someone, we can look at the issue of gay marriage and the separation of Church and State. Gay marriage advocates are not seeking to change any religious body's theology or practice of marriage. They only seek to add gay or lesbian couples to the list of people eligible to access the civil institution of marriage.

Opponents of gay marriage, especially religious opponents, argue in the media that the State is violating their constitutionally protected right to exercise their religion without interference from the State. They argue that the State is overstepping its bounds by "changing the definition" of marriage and imposing it on religious communities. The facts are clear that this is anything but the case.

In the states where marriage between same-gender partners has become legal, it has been made very clear that no religious body or any particular clergyperson will ever have to authorize, solemnize, or preside over a same-gender marriage. (Indeed, no clergyperson is ever required to marry *any* particular couple against his or her wishes or theology.) In New Hampshire, as the same-sex marriage law was being written, this already-provided protection was restated in the legislative bill itself. HB 436 reads in part: "Affirmation of Freedom of Religion in Marriage. Members of the clergy as described in RSA 457:31 or other persons otherwise authorized under law to solemnize a marriage shall not be obligated or otherwise required by law to officiate at any particular civil marriage or religious rite of marriage in violation of their right to free exercise of religion protected by the First Amendment to the United States Constitution or by part I, article 5 of the New Hampshire constitution."

That means that no religious body will ever have to bless or sanctify a legal marriage between two people of the same gender if doing so goes against its policy. Period. The agreement to act as an agent of the State in officiating at marriages is at the discretion of the clergyperson or religious institution she or he represents. If the church, synagogue, mosque, or temple does not recognize or sanction the holy union of two people of the same gender, it simply declines to officiate at such a marriage. Appeals and arguments against gay marriage based on the violation of "Church and State" are simply red herrings meant to inspire fear and opposition to this change.

I would go further. I believe that religious opposition

to same-gender marriage is an example of violation of the separation of Church and State in the *other* direction. Usually when we talk about the separation of Church and State, we are concerned that the State might impinge on the life and internal workings of religion, or one particular brand of religion. Is not the attempt of religious institutions to block passage of the right to marry for gay and lesbian couples an example of the Church trying to meddle in the rightful business of the State? Is this not an example of religious bodies trying to impose their will on the civil state?

What would happen if, say, the citizenry of the United States were to become majority Muslim, and Muslim lawmakers were to change the law and require every adult female to wear a head covering or burqa? Wouldn't Christians and Jews and other non-Muslims be outraged that a religious majority was imposing its will on the minority population, and wouldn't we brand that as the interference of religion with the State? Wouldn't it be argued that that constituted an unlawful interference of religion with what is actually the State's rights? I certainly think so.

So isn't the religious opposition to the State's efforts to regulate the civil institution of marriage also such an instance of the Church interfering with the State and thereby violating the separation principle? The religious institutions of this nation have every right to regulate what marriages they will and won't add their blessing to, but no religious body has the right to tell the State who can and who can't be married.

I think the separation of Church and State has a rightful and appropriate place in this gay marriage debate. But defending that separation means arguing for the State's right to regulate who is and who is not eligible to avail themselves of that civil institution. To let religious institutions interfere would indeed be a violation of the long-held and revered separation of Church and State.

We can move to legalize same-gender civil marriage without harming any religious institution or dictating any change to the beliefs and practices of any faith. Religious opposition to civil marriage for same-gender couples is irrelevant to the civil, public debate. You're opposed to gay marriage on religious grounds? Fine! Don't authorize your clergy to act as an agent of the State in any such unions. But don't deprive the rest of us, who believe that such rites are good and holy, of our constitutional right to practice our own freedom of religion. We don't live in a theocracy where some one understanding of religion and faith dictates what the State will and will not do. This religious argument against the right to marry for gay and lesbian couples is simply bogus. And unconstitutional. Religious belief should have no bearing whatsoever on the legal right to marry.

CHAPTER 9

Don't Children Need a Mother
and a Father?

My daughters were four and eight years old when I came out to them, explaining the reason their mother and I were separating. I asked the older, Jamee, if she knew what gay people were. "Sure!" she said. "Most boys like girls, and most girls like boys, but some boys like boys, and some girls like girls." Jamee knew that our housekeeper and beloved nanny was lesbian. "Well," I said, "Daddy has come to understand that I'm one of those boys who likes boys."

I then read her a children's book I had found, *Jenny Lives with Eric and Martin,* by Susanne Bösche, published in Denmark in 1981. (Such books were nearly impossible to find among American publishers in 1986!) It unselfconsciously told the story, in pictures and words, of two men who live together with the daughter of one of them. It showed amazingly commonplace scenes of a family—playing outdoors, eating meals, going to the market, reading stories at bedtime. It showed her mom coming to visit. It showed her angry, pensive, and joyous. The only thing remarkable about this book is that Jenny lives her young life with her dad and his male partner.

After I put Jamee to bed that night, as I was leaving her room, she called out to me, "Dad, someday I hope *you* find an Eric!" I knew in my heart that everything would be all right.

As Jamee and Ella grew up, they took different tacks about sharing the fact that they had two dads. I had met Mark nearly a year and a half after separating from my wife, and he came into the girls' lives when they were nearly six and ten. Jamee was more private about whom she shared this fact of her life with, telling her best friends and bringing them to our house for sleepovers and good times.

Ella, on the other hand, was much more open and public about her gay dads. When in sixth grade, at a small private school tucked in the shadow of New Hampshire's Mount Monadnock, Ella and her class experienced some antigay comments by a visiting teacher. Ella talked first with her classmates, each of whom she had previously made aware of her two gay dads, about how hurtful his comments had been to her and how unfair to her dads. Then she went to the head of the school with her anger. Together, they planned a response. The teacher was asked to come back to the school and face this class of sixth graders who meant to hold him accountable for what he had said. He apologized for his remarks.

Uncoached by me, Jamee and Ella, separately, wrote their college entrance essays on what they had learned from being raised by their two gay dads. Among those learnings were an understanding of prejudice and the pain it causes its targets, a tolerance for those who are different, and an appreciation of the diversity of humankind. Twenty-five years later, they continue to be my greatest blessings, my close and beloved friends, and that of which I am most proud.

Isn't marriage for raising children, and don't children do best when they have a mother and a father? This assumption bears some looking into. However true it may have been in the past that marriage is primarily for the raising of children, it is no longer the understanding—either of the culture or of the Church. And the question of whether it is better for children to be raised by two people, and whether those two people more appropriately and more healthfully should be male *and* female, needs to be examined in light of present-day practice and understanding. Indeed, the questions themselves may point to bias and prejudice on the part of the heterosexual majority.

Even the Church (at least major segments of it) has long since abandoned the notion that marriage itself is exclusively, or even primarily, for the raising of children. Indeed, the opening of The Episcopal Church's prayer book service "The Celebration and Blessing of a Marriage" contains these words: "The union of husband and wife in heart, body, and mind is intended by God for their mutual joy; for the help and comfort given one another in prosperity and adversity; and, when it is God's will, for the procreation of children and their nurture in the knowledge and love of the Lord."

The order in which these purposes of marriage are listed is not accidental. Over a period of years, and by the time of the publication of the latest Book of Common Prayer—1979—the raising of children as a purpose of marriage had taken third place in theological thinking to the mutual joy of the couple and to their mutual help and comfort through thick and thin. This change in priorities of purpose reflects the change in understanding among people of faith in line with society's purpose of greater stability.

First and foremost, marriage is for the couple themselves. We understand that uniting with another person in marriage is the deepest expression of love and commitment two people can show each other. Centuries before, as we have seen, love was hardly a necessary component of the process leading to marriage. It was, sometimes, a wonderful by-product of such a union but certainly not a consideration prior to the marriage. Now, in this day and age, romantic love is pretty much an essential component in anyone's understanding of marriage.

At least in this country, each party to the marriage must have given meaningful consent to the union. In some cultures and nations this is not necessarily true, although even in many "arranged" marriages, the bride and groom have given their consent to marry the person of their parents' choice. My husband, Mark, recalls that in returning to the United States from a two-year Peace Corps posting in Côte d'Ivoire, he encountered a young man in Algeria who was betrothed to a young woman he had never met. When asked how he felt about that, this young Muslim man said he was absolutely confident that his mother had chosen the perfect mate for him. Consent comes in many forms.

Second in this ordering of the priorities and purposes of marriage is the notion of commitment, come what may. As part of the "Declaration of Consent," each party to the marriage answers in the affirmative to the question: "Will you love him, comfort him, honor and keep him, in sickness and in health; and, forsaking all others, be faithful to him as long as you both shall live?" Then in the vows themselves, the bride and groom promise each other "to have and to hold from this day forward, for better for worse, for richer for poorer, in sickness and in health, to love and to cherish, until we are parted by death." This is all in service to society's desire for stability.

Then, and only then, does the priority of children get listed as one of the purposes of marriage. And even then, there is the proviso "if it is God's will." It is also interesting to note that it is not just the procreation of children but their "nurture in the knowledge and love of the Lord" that is honored. It is the recognition that marriage is the stable environment in which children find their optimum support. This articulation honors the possibility of adoption for those couples who cannot or choose not to conceive the children they will be raising.

Most heterosexual couples, of course, do choose to conceive the children they raise. But it is significant that the Church, in the liturgical act of marrying the couple, does not state anything about who physically procreates the children or how. Those couples who choose not to raise children as a part of their marriage still enjoy the primary purposes of "mutual joy," commitment, and stability promised in marriage. There is no discrimination against or withholding of the sacrament of marriage from those couples who cannot or choose not to have children.

Even the most severe critics of marriage for gay or lesbian people honor the practice of adoption. The world has too many children who, for one reason or another, find themselves without parents. Gay male couples seem especially willing to adopt "problematic" orphans—those who are older, those who are severely disabled or have AIDS, and those considered virtually "unadoptable." Most everyone would claim that these children will do better in a home and family than in an institution. However, the opposition to same-gender couples has led some denominations like the Roman Catholic Church to choose to leave these children in institutional care rather than facilitate their adoption by same-gender couples.

So, is it detrimental to a child to be raised by a same-gender couple?

There is one thing common to all adoptions, be they by a heterosexual or a homosexual couple: the adopted child is wanted. Couples who choose to adopt by definition have to be intentional about wanting a child. The adoption process is a long and tedious one, requiring enormous amounts of time, commitment, and (usually) money. Indeed, most couples find adoption to be an exhausting and trying process. It is not for the faint of heart.

Contrast that to the procreation of children by heterosexual couples. While many of these couples decide it is the right time to have children and set about "getting pregnant," there are also many children conceived "by accident," that is, without a conscious choice to do so. Some of these conceptions are clearly undesired—hence the disturbing number of abortions performed. Most of these conceptions, especially among the young and unmarried, are the result of choosing to have intercourse without birth control. Some are conceived in the passion of the moment, seemingly oblivious to the reality that a child might be conceived. Some are the result of a man (or boy) forcing himself on his wife (or girlfriend), pushing her against her will to have sex with him without contraceptive prevention for his own physical pleasure, with no thought to a resulting pregnancy.

Adoptive couples, however, have months and months to consider if this is what they really want. Working through an exhaustive process, these couples are required to open their private lives to representatives of the adoption agency who do a thorough "home study" to determine the appropriateness and health of the couple/family. These would-be parents are not finding themselves "stuck" with a child they'd rather not have had; instead, they have carefully and thoughtfully decided to raise a child. This is as true for gay or lesbian adoptive couples as it is for straight couples. These children are wanted! Already, these children have a leg up on life, in an environment that welcomes them.

Not coincidentally, this process is usually very expensive. It generally means that adoptive parents are more likely to have the financial resources that make a child's life more secure. Though these children may have been conceived in an atmosphere of poverty, either in this country or abroad, their adoptive homes will, by definition, not be so.

All of this is to say that adoptive parents, be they gay or straight, do not take their parenthood for granted. There is a spirit of appreciation and joy that surrounds this child from the very beginning. Adoption is the successful end product of a long-sought-after reality of parenthood. This can be nothing but positive for the adopted child. All adoptions by gay or lesbian couples share this reality with heterosexual adoptive parents.

But critics of adoption by gay couples will often raise what they see to be negative consequences of having two parents of the same gender. First, in an objection designed to sound sympathetic and caring, it is alleged that these children will be subjected to teasing, bullying, and discrimination because they have two dads or two moms. That is, sadly, true. They may indeed be on the receiving end of such hateful behavior. Studies show that such children are more likely to be bullied and taunted at school. They may not know how to navigate the waters of explaining that they have gay parents to school officials who may be insensitive or negative toward such a family.

But isn't this a case of "blaming the *victim*"?! This is a problem brought on not by the gay or lesbian parents, or by their children, but by the bigotry coming from external sources. And besides, we don't argue that African-Americans should not have children because they will be the targets of racism. We assume that African-American parents, who have experienced racism themselves, will be able to assist their children in resisting this discrimination and the self-doubt that is often its consequence. Gay and lesbian parents have undoubtedly experienced discrimination and even hatred as a result of being gay. Who better to help their children in understanding and countering this behavior on the part of others?

In addition, the stigma for children raised by same-gender parents is lessened if those parents are legally married. Gay couples themselves often find it difficult to explain to a hospital official or a magistrate that they were joined in a civil union and have rights under such a legal arrangement. But if they are able to say "We're married," everyone knows what that means. Children find it much easier to understand for themselves and to explain to others that their parents are married. End of sentence. No six-year-old is going to be able to explain to her first-grade teacher that her parents are not really married, but rather they have legal documents that give them some of the legal protections they need in order to be a family. Marriage turns out to be the clear and understandable way the child knows himself or herself to be part of a family. This means less stigma for a possibly stigmatized situation.

The real reason behind the "sympathetic" concern over discrimination is that opponents of gay marriage believe a household headed by two people of the same gender is just sick, unhealthy, and psychologically damaging. It has been forty years since the American Psychiatric Association removed homosexuality from the *Diagnostic and Statistical Manual of Mental Disorders.* Yet many continue to believe that being gay is an illness. Therefore, to put children in a gay household is to plunge them into a sick atmosphere, harmful to their development and happiness.

The facts show otherwise.

The sociologists Judith Stacey of New York University and Timothy Biblarz of the University of Southern California spent five years reviewing eighty-one studies of one- and two-parent families, including gay, lesbian, and heterosexual couples. The results of their research appeared in the *Journal of Marriage and Family* in February 2010. "No research supports the widely held conviction that the gender of parents matters for child well-being," they conclude. "Children being raised by same-gender parents, on most all of the measures that we care about, self-esteem, school performance, social adjustment and so on, seem to be doing just fine and, in most cases, are statistically indistinguishable from kids raised by married moms and dads on these measures," Biblarz says.

Stacey and Biblarz end with their conclusions:

The entrenched conviction that children need both a mother and a father inflames culture wars over single motherhood, divorce, gay marriage, and gay parenting. Research to date, however, does not support this claim. Contrary to popular belief, studies have not shown that "compared to all other family forms, families headed by married, biological parents are best for children" (Popenoe, quoted in Center for Marriage and Family, p. 1). Research has not identified any gender-exclusive parenting abilities (with the partial exception of lactation)...

Current claims that children need both a mother and father are spurious because they attribute to the gender of parents benefits that correlate primarily with the number and marital status of a child's parents since infancy. *At this point no research supports the widely held conviction that the gender of parents matters for child well-being* [emphasis added].

Michael Rosenfeld, a Stanford sociologist, published a study in *Demography* in August 2010 showing that there is essentially no difference in educational achievement between children raised by heterosexual parents and those raised by parents who identify themselves as same-gender partners. Rosenfeld's study of the 2000 census indicates only a slight edge in academic achievement by children raised in a heterosexual family, summarizing that the difference between the groups pretty much vanishes when taking into account that the heterosexual couples were slightly more educated and wealthier than most gay parents. *"The census data show that having parents who are the same gender is not in itself any disadvantage to children,"* he said (emphasis added). "Parents' income and education are the biggest indicators of a child's success. Family structure is a minor determinant."

Nanette Gartrell, M.D., and Henny Bos, Ph.D., undertook the "US National Longitudinal Lesbian Family Study: Psychological Adjustment of 17-Year-Old Adolescents," whose results were published by the American Academy of Pediatrics. The objective of the study was "to document the psychological adjustment of adolescents who were conceived through donor insemination by lesbian mothers who enrolled before these offspring were born in the largest, longest running, prospective, longitudinal study of same-sex-parented families." This study had an astounding 93 percent retention rate of those who participated from the beginning.

According to their mothers' reports, the 17-year-old daughters and sons of lesbian mothers were rated significantly higher in social, school/academic, and total competence and significantly lower in social problems, rule-breaking, aggressive, and externalizing problem behavior than their age-matched counterparts in Achenbach's normative sample of American youth. Within the lesbian family sample, no Child Behavior Checklist differences were found among adolescent offspring who were conceived by known, as-yet-unknown, and permanently unknown donors or between offspring whose mothers were still together and offspring whose mothers had separated.

The study concluded:

Adolescents who have been reared in lesbian-mother families since birth demonstrate healthy psychological adjustment. These findings have implications for the clinical care of adolescents and for pediatricians who are consulted on matters that pertain to same-sex parenting. (*Pediatrics* 126, no. 1 [2010])

The American Academy of Child and Adolescent Psychiatry perhaps best sums up this research in its Gay, Lesbian, Bisexual or Transgender Parents Policy Statement, adopted in June 1999:

The basis on which all decisions relating to custody and parental rights should rest on the best interest of the child. Lesbian, gay, and bisexual individuals historically have faced more rigorous scrutiny than heterosexuals regarding their rights to be or become parents.

There is no evidence to suggest or support that parents with a gay, lesbian, or bisexual orientation are per se different from or deficient in parenting skills, child-centered concerns and parent-child attachments, when compared to parents with a heterosexual orientation. It has long been established that a homosexual orientation is not related to psychopathology, and there is no basis on which to assume that a parental homosexual orientation will increase likelihood of or induce a homosexual orientation in the child.

Outcome studies of children raised by parents with a homosexual or bisexual orientation, when compared to heterosexual parents, show no greater degree of instability in the parental relationship or developmental dysfunction in children.

Now, these may seem like dry statistics, but let's be clear. There are arguments being made against gay couples and gay marriage on the basis that such unions are inherently unhealthy environments for children, and none of the research shows this to be the case. One can argue against the facts and the research, but doing so is purely an act of bias and prejudice.

Aside from the sometimes visceral aversion to the notion

of homosexuality in general, at the center of this bias and prejudice is the notion that the children of gay or lesbian parents will have insufficient access to and modeling from adults whose gender is opposite that of their parents. How will a boy who grows up with two moms know what it means to be a man?!

Just as gay and lesbian couples are intentional (by necessity) about having children in the first place, they tend to be intentional about bringing role models of the opposite gender into their children's lives, especially if the child's gender is opposite that of his or her gay parents. The children of a gay couple are part of a larger family, just as children are in the families of heterosexual parents. Grandparents, aunts, uncles, and their spouses enrich the lives of these children, just as they do in other families. Add to that their godparents, friends, and other supportive people in the lives of their parents. We don't seem to worry too much about those being raised by a single parent or wonder aloud if they will be too affected by the presence of only one gender in the household.

Fear seems to be a big influence in these attitudes. But fear of what? What is it that opponents of gay marriage/parenting fear these children won't learn? Are we afraid that boys raised by lesbians won't learn to cross their legs by resting one ankle on the other knee in a "manly" fashion? Or that girls raised by two gay men won't learn to cross their legs at the ankles? Are they afraid that boys will turn out "effeminate"? Or that girls will be "tomboys"?

Such worries seem absurd at best, especially in a time when gender expression among all children has become more fluid and broad. More and more, parents of all stripes are allowing their children simply to be who they are, not overly obsessing on their mannerisms and gestures. If a boy wants to play with dolls and play house, let him! If a girl wants to do science experiments and play in the mud with tractors, let her! Besides, all parents I know, including me, have experienced their children's resistance to being channeled into "gender appropriate" behavior against their will! It's going to be what it's going to be.

I suspect that the real resistance to same-gender parenting comes down to the fear that gay parents will make their children gay. Many opponents of gay marriage are too savvy to state it so boldly, but I suspect that such a fear is close to the surface for many, all evidence to the contrary. The fact is that the children of gay parents are no more and no less likely to be gay themselves than are their heterosexually raised counterparts. The evidence simply does not support such fears.

What *is* true and predictable, however, is that if any of the children raised by gay or lesbian parents do discover themselves to be gay, they will not grow up with the fear of being rejected by their parents. This, of course, is the single most powerful fear operating in the minds and hearts of kids who suspect they might be gay: rejection by their parents. While home is supposed to be the one place "they have to take you in," the fact is that huge numbers of teenagers are thrown out of their heterosexually parented families when it is revealed (or discovered) that they are gay.

This is no small problem, caused by heterosexual parents who believe what they have been told, either by the culture or by their religion, that homosexuality is wrong and perverse. Nicholas Ray edited a 2006 report showing that 20 to 40 percent of homeless youth identified as lesbian, gay, bisexual, or transgender. This study, *Lesbian, Gay, Bisexual, and Transgender Youth: An Epidemic of Homelessness,* sponsored by the National Gay and Lesbian Task Force Policy Institute and the National Coalition for the Homeless, reviewed the data showing that 26 percent of teens who come out to their parent(s) are thrown out of their homes. They wind up living with a relative or friend, or living on the streets of our cities. And like heterosexual homeless teens, they often resort to selling their bodies in sex work just to survive.

Having gay or lesbian parents won't make kids gay or lesbian themselves. There will be no deficiencies in these children's growth and development as a result of the gender or sexual orientation of their parents. If children's gay or lesbian parents are legally married, their lives might be made simpler to understand by their heterosexual peers and adult teachers and supervisors. And a child who grows up with gay or lesbian parents is apt to be more tolerant of difference, more sympathetic to those who for whatever reason don't fit in, and more welcoming of diversity.

One last argument for the right to *marry* for gay or

lesbian couples, which may seem a bit odd, is the right to *divorce*. While legal marriage brings certain benefits and rights, it also brings the protection afforded by legal divorce. If a couple is legally married and that marriage falls apart, not only are both of them protected by that legal status, but so are their children. The court will see to it that the two adults seeking a divorce will care appropriately for the children of that marriage, maintain financial support for the children, and ensure access to visitation and some sharing of legal custody. This is a vital protection for children that, absent legal marriage, is often left to informal arrangements between two people who may be angry with each other and not terribly open to any kind of cooperative arrangement. If such a difficult and unresolvable situation develops, resorting to the courts can be costly in terms of money and time. If one of the partners is the biological mother or father, the other partner has a difficult time documenting his or her participation in the child's life. The legal protection and processes provided to married couples in divorce turn out to be a significant contribution to the security and prosperity of the children of a marriage. This would argue for legal marriage for gay and lesbian couples, for the benefit not only of the couples but of their children.

In short, there is no good reason to think that children are at any disadvantage in being raised by gay or lesbian couples. Marriage turns out to be good not only for gay or lesbian couples but for the raising, nurture, and protection of their children. Arguments and opinions to the contrary, no matter how firmly held or loudly proclaimed, are simply not based in fact. Yes, marriage is (for many) about raising a family. No, there are no detriments to the children based simply on their parents' orientation or gender.

CHAPTER 10

Is This About Civil Rights or Getting Approval for Questionable Behavior?

M y husband, Mark, and I are aboard a US Airways flight back to America. We're approaching our entryway into the United States. This is the part of the trip that I always dread. It's a small thing, but disturbing nevertheless. The flight attendant comes down the aisle with immigration/customs forms. And the words out of his mouth are "One per family."

When the flight attendant gets to us, he hands us *each* a form—because the federal government doesn't recognize that we are a family. Never mind that we've been together for twenty-four years. The fact that we travel with legal documents certifying that we are legally married in the State of New Hampshire is irrelevant. In the eyes of the U.S. government, to which I vow allegiance and pay taxes, we are two wholly unrelated people traveling together. Our marriage doesn't count. Our family isn't a family, not really.

Sitting across the aisle is a young attractive couple, returning from their honeymoon. They have been married all of one week! And *one* immigration form will suffice for them. Because, unlike us, they are a family.

Critics of the movement for equal civil rights for lesbian, gay, bisexual, and transgender people will sometimes assert that this struggle is simply not a civil rights movement. Rather, it seems to them, this is just a group of people seeking status and recognition for their questionable behavior. This objection/accusation needs some parsing to see it as the prejudicial opinion it represents.

Civil rights are different from disagreements of opinion and perspective. Civil rights are the area of inquiry as to the legitimate and equal claims of all American citizens on the government, based on the constitutionally protected status of its citizens. Civil rights have to do with fair treatment before the law and the reasonable expectation of citizens that they will not be discriminated against based on individual prejudice—even prejudice shared by a majority of the citizenry.

Indeed, it is precisely the "tyranny of the majority" from which the Constitution, including its Bill of Rights, promises to protect a minority. If African-Americans had had to wait for a majority of citizens to agree that they were being unfairly discriminated against, Jim Crow laws might still be on the books. If a majority of Americans had had to agree that women were being discriminated against in unfair employment practices, less qualified men would still be able to be hired or promoted over more qualified women without recourse in the courts. If disabled Americans had waited for a majority of the citizenry to notice that physically handicapped people were paying a price for non-accessibility, we wouldn't have access ramps, elevators, and wheelchair-accessible curbs and crosswalks.

It is difficult for a majority to see, let alone sympathize with, a practice that discriminates against a minority. It's not unlike trying to get a fish to understand the concept of water! It is simply the medium in which the fish resides, requiring no cognition of the water that supports it. Discrimination—not just individual, but systemic—is the "water" in which the majority swims, and unless something happens to bring that discrimination into the view and consciousness of the majority, nothing will change, because the majority hardly, if ever, even notices it. That is why African-Americans took to the streets in the 1960s, why women voiced their concerns in the 1970s, and why disabled people banded together in the 1980s to promote the Americans with Disabilities Act, which passed in 1990.

Let's be clear here. We are not necessarily talking about changing the opinions or feelings of the majority. Just because Jim Crow laws came off the books in the 1960s does not mean that racism ended, personal or systemic. But that action did provide some relief and legal recourse to African-Americans who had paid dearly for the color of their skin, even a hundred years after the Emancipation Proclamation. Just because Title IX funding for women's sports became a reality, sexism has not disappeared in the workplace, on the playing field, or in individual relationships. Just because we have more handicapped-accessible public spaces does not mean that reasonable accommodation of physical handicaps occurs in all the places it should. But these were all important steps forward.

Among young thinkers and scholars today, the concept of intersectionality is a huge topic of discussion. The fact of the matter is that while specific discrimination against particular minorities is different in form, substance, and function, there is an astounding similarity between the ways in which these discriminations occur. The dynamics of discrimination by a majority over a minority are profoundly similar.

Let's look at the way discrimination happens. Discrimination is much more than prejudice. Anyone can be prejudiced against anyone else and any other group. There's no law against disdain or hate. But when the discriminating majority has the power to enact their disdain (or condemnation or mere underestimation of the burden being perpetrated on the minority) into law and practice their condemnation in the workplace, we have discrimination. An "ism" happens when a prejudice combines with the power to put it into practice, in formal and informal ways, to the detriment of those being discriminated against.

Racism is the combination of the prejudice that says it is better to be white than to be a person of color with the power to enforce, or at least legally allow, that prejudice to be ensconced in the laws of the land. At a gathering at the White House, President Barack Obama noted that when his father was his age, he wouldn't have been allowed to eat at most lunch counters in Washington, D.C. African-Americans were not accorded equality in public accommodation. Sexism is the combination of the prejudice that maintains it is better to be male than to be female with the power to enforce, or at least legally allow, that prejudice to be acted out in the workplace and elsewhere in the culture, without any legal recourse. We live in a country where equal pay for equal work is still not a reality, but at least there is legal recourse in individual, and even some class action, cases.

When it comes to the issue of equal civil rights for lesbian, gay, bisexual, and transgender people, we are not talking about homophobia. "Homophobia" is a word I almost never use, because it's a conversation stopper. It's hard to continue a conversation, never mind to teach someone anything, when you've just called him a bigot! And while homophobia (variously described as fear and/ or hatred of homosexuals) is to be resisted whenever and wherever it occurs, we are *not* talking about people's *feelings* when we talk about civil rights. Changing people's minds and hearts about their *feelings* toward the gay community is not what civil rights are concerned with. The question regarding civil rights is, "Is the *system* set up in a way that benefits heterosexual people at the expense of homosexual people?" And is such a discrepancy legitimate, defensible, and constitutional?

The systemic "ism" we are confronting here is heterosexism. We would be well served to begin using this word to describe the struggle in which we in the LGBT community and all Americans who seek justice are engaged. While we would like to change people's minds and hearts and feelings about us, that is a long and gradual endeavor. This is a civil rights issue because we are fighting to ensure that we are not systemically discriminated against in the laws, the tax structure, and the other benefits and responsibilities offered to the majority of American citizens. This is a systemic debate, not an emotional one—which is hard to see when emotions fill up most of the airtime given to this struggle and the opposition to it.

Heterosexism is an enshrinement of prejudice against gay people and our relationships into the laws and practices of our governmental and societal institutions. Some are obvious: Until recently, and only after seventeen years of living with the policy, gay and lesbian people were not able to serve openly in the military under "Don't Ask, Don't Tell." Until fairly recently, openly gay government workers, by virtue of their sexual orientation, were seen as security risks and could not obtain security clearances, necessary to certain jobs. Most states have absolutely no protections against discrimination against gay people who want to rent an apartment, eat a meal, or hold a job. Without such protections, LGBT people are at risk for overt discrimination without recourse.

Beyond discrimination based on sexual orientation, there is the more specific discrimination based on access to the institution of marriage. Society has a stake in stable familial relationships. Generally stable relationships tend to support a generally stable society. To that end, the society, through its government, grants certain privileges based on the institution of marriage, considering it a good investment in the society at large.

The government doesn't particularly care about the manner in which two people are married. You can be married by a justice of the peace without mention of religion or faith. In most states, *any* person may obtain a one-day license to officiate at a wedding, be he or she a parent of the bride or groom, a relative, a friend, or a complete stranger. There are no prescribed vows to be taken, and there is no effort whatsoever by the government to manage or control the promises made in such vows. Indeed, no vows need be taken at all! What makes a man and a woman married in the eyes of the State is the signature of a duly authorized person on the marriage license returned to the local magistrate of that jurisdiction, attesting that these two people are now married.

And what does the legally married couple receive in

return for their buy-in to the institution of marriage? Tax benefits accrue to the new couple immediately—note the number of marriages that take place on New Year's Eve, presumably for the purpose of filing a joint return for that entire year! Unlike members of unmarried couples who are treated as strangers to each other at the death of one of them, a spouse in a married couple is welcome to pass along much if not all of his or her wealth to the surviving spouse undiminished by taxes. If the spouse dies without a will, the entire estate passes to the surviving spouse automatically. Married couples, and their children if they have any, are given preferential rates in membership fees at country clubs, gyms, and civic organizations, not available to non-legally married couples and families.

If the husband of a married couple is in the hospital, there is no lengthy grilling of his wife about whether she should have access to her sick or injured spouse. If the husband is comatose, there is no question that his wife gets to make health-care decisions for him. If one of them dies, the surviving spouse gets to make decisions about funeral arrangements, how the body is disposed of, and where the spouse is buried. If the marriage ends in divorce, the legal proceeding and agreement ensure that certain responsibilities are fulfilled—principally the support of the children born to the marriage or adopted into it. A spouse who is dependent on the other spouse financially is entitled to a share of the common wealth of the marriage, and sometimes to ongoing support from the greater wage earner. To put it bluntly, the society sees it in its own self-interest to make *being* married and *staying* married so advantageous as to make couples think long and hard about dissolving a marriage and forfeiting their privileges, both financial and otherwise.

These privileges are granted immediately upon marriage. Britney Spears can get drunk and find her way to a Las Vegas wedding chapel with a man, and voilà, they're married, and all the privileges of marriage accrue to them in an instant. Never mind that they dissolve the union days later. That doesn't prevent either of them from doing the same thing again. As many times as they like. And each time, these privileges will immediately become theirs for as long as they are married.

Yet at the same time, a same-gender couple who may have been together for twenty, thirty, or forty years have none of these benefits. Their lives, finances, and families may have been totally integrated for decades, but none of these legal privileges are theirs. Those with the financial resources to do so may spend several thousand dollars putting in place legal documents that accomplish some of these benefits, in terms of health-care decisions, power of attorney, and so on. But many same-gender couples are unable to do so, and some are not aware that they can accomplish some of these protections with legal help. Many discover belatedly how unprotected they are when they are in the middle of a medical crisis and find themselves completely vulnerable to the rules of the system.

The issue of "Are homosexuals seeking approval for their questionable behavior?" in seeking their full and equal civil rights begs the question of to what extent the government is concerned with behavior. Clearly, the government is interested in behavior that has ill effects on other citizens, and the prisons are full of those who robbed, defrauded, hurt, or killed their fellow citizens. It is part of the purpose of government to enact laws that forbid provable harm to someone else and to punish those who violate those laws.

But the extent to which government restricts or controls private behavior is less clear. This has real relevance to the issue of marriage. Yes, for many years, many states had laws prohibiting sodomy. What most people don't know is that many of these laws prohibited not only sexual intimacy between people of the same gender but certain kinds of sexual intimacy between heterosexual, even married, couples as well. The fact that the laws were never enforced against opposite-gender couples led many to understand, erroneously, that it was only gay sex that was illegal. Those laws have now been declared unconstitutional by the U.S. Supreme Court and stricken from the books.

The fact is that the State has no particular interest in what two people do within the confines of their relationship. If it were the government's job to police the behavior of mutually consenting couples in their sex lives, within the context of marriage, we might see the following questions on the application for a marriage license: What will be the nature of your sexual intimacy? Will you be celibate, even though married? Will you be sexually intimate frequently or seldom? Will you be active or passive in your sexual relationship, or both? Will you be physically faithful to each other? What will you do if one of you is not? Will you use sex toys in your lovemaking? Will you dress in leather? Will you use whips and chains and role-playing? Will you dress in lingerie? Will there be spanking? Will there be oral sex? By one, or both? Will you have anal intercourse?

If the government were actually interested in the behaviors that go on within a marriage, these questions would be asked of straight couples who seek to be married. And all of the above-mentioned practices and behaviors go on in at least some heterosexual marriages. But the fact is that the State has no interest in whether these practices take place within a marriage, or else we would be asking.

So why are we focused on sexual practices and behaviors when it comes to same-gender marriage? And is it not only inconsistent but inappropriate to ask these questions of one minority group of citizens while not asking them of the majority?

My guess is that gay sex may be every bit as boring as straight sex! Conversely, straight sex may be as kinky, naughty, and wild as gay sex. We know that anal intercourse is practiced in straight relationships (not just gay), with a quarter of all heterosexual couples having tried it at least once, and 10 percent of the heterosexual population report having anal sex on a regular basis.

I'm not sure anyone knows the reasons for this focus on

gay sexual practices as an objection to gay marriage, but I will hazard some guesses: It is usually the sexual practices of gay men, not lesbians, that cause the biggest emotional reaction, especially among heterosexual men. Men are not used to being treated and objectified as sexual objects (after all, that's what many red-blooded all-American men do to women), and the legitimization of homosexuality means that they might themselves be objectified as sex objects. Such men find this infuriating and demeaning and shameful (not unlike most women on the receiving end of such objectification). In response, some men—especially young men whose sexuality is still being formed—pick up a baseball bat and smash the skull of the gay man who looked at him a little too long, a little too suggestively, screaming "faggot" all the while. In court, the defense used in such a hate crime is "He made a pass at me." And yet men make passes at women all the time! Homosexuality, it turns out, is a problem, largely and mostly, for heterosexual men, not heterosexual women. Homosexuality in men turns out to be a perceived threat to male privilege and patriarchy.

The focus on the sexual behavior of gay men and lesbians is used as an argument against marriage equality precisely because it is historically and traditionally taboo, and therefore emotionally charged. Frankly, the repulsion that some heterosexuals feel when they think about gay sex should be instructive to them: it is confirmation that they are heterosexually inclined, and it should give them a window into the same sort of "ick" feeling that some homosexuals feel at the thought of having sex with a person of the opposite sex. It is confirmation that most of us are hardwired about the objects of our affection, fantasy, and love. Is it possible for us all to learn that sexual attraction is not right and wrong but simply different?

The argument for marriage equality for all our citizens is not about behavior. There are certain behaviors in marriages, whether same- or opposite-gender marriages, that are unhealthy, inappropriate, and even abusive—and they are to be resisted. But the State's interests in *civil* marriage do not focus on behaviors. They focus on the consensual willingness to enter into a legally binding agreement about mutual responsibilities—within marriage and, if that marriage ends in divorce, after marriage.

This struggle is not about certain sexual practices that are abhorrent to some, because those practices are engaged in by both homosexuals and heterosexuals. This debate is about the civil, legal right to marry for all our citizens. It's about the freedom to marry the person of one's choice.

CHAPTER 11

God Believes in Love

As I write this last chapter, my mom sits in her wheelchair or rocker, unable to walk or even lift her foot up onto the wheelchair's footrest by herself. She eats with an apron-sized bib around her neck, using specially angled silverware that gives her a better chance of actually getting food to her mouth. Increasingly, my dad feeds her. Indeed, my dad does virtually everything for her now. He gets her up in the middle of the night—several times a night—for the arduous process of getting her out of bed, into the bathroom, and back again. He's hardly gone back to sleep when she needs to go again. They're both eighty-six years old.

They get cranky with each other. My mother now speaks only in a whisper. My father needs hearing aids but refuses to try them. She is irritated that he can't hear her, and he wishes she would just speak up. Sometimes he is impatient. Sometimes she is just so very tired. Still, there they are, 24/7, continuing their life together.

Mom needs to be in the nursing home part of their progressive care facility. She was there for a while, but my father missed her and was worried about whether she was getting good care (meaning round-the-clock, one-on-one attention). He said to me, "I just can't stand the thought of your mother sitting in a dirty diaper, for who knows how long, waiting for someone to come change her. It's my job to take care of her, and that's what I'm gonna do, until I can't do it anymore." And so he is.

For more than sixty-five years, longer than some people live, my parents have been married. They were married as soon as my father returned from World War II. They were both twenty years old. They were poor and barely educated. And scarcely over twenty-one, they had me, an extra burden on an already stressed family. And yet that family has endured for more than sixty-five years. They absorbed the shock of their firstborn's coming-out at age thirty-nine. And against all odds, their love for me trumped all that they had learned in Sunday-after-Sunday Bible study. Or perhaps it was that in spite of what they had been taught about homosexuality, they had actually learned from their Bible that in the end God's love wins.

I don't know if anyone can adequately define the mystery of marriage, but I know it when I see it. My parents' marriage stands as a tribute to the idea of marriage, its faithful commitment and its until-death-do-us-part tenacity. This "fragile" institution is remarkably resilient, it seems to me. But why it works and how it works are still a mystery. Even when you account for real commitment, hard work, and a bit of luck, nothing really explains how the relationship of marriage can be so strong and so life-giving, except for grace. Grace is that blessing which comes as a gift, unearned and undeserved. For people of faith, that grace is God's promised gift to those who commit themselves to each other in marriage.

God is all about love. Whatever is at the center of the universe, whatever gives meaning to creaturely existence, whatever we mean by "God," it is all about love. There is no more fundamental belief among people of faith.

Many adjectives are used in the holy texts of major religions to describe God—what God is like, as experienced by human beings, what God is apt to favor, what God abhors. In Christianity, God is defined quite simply in the New Testament's First Letter of John: "Love is from God; everyone who loves is born of God and knows God. Whoever does not love does not know God, for God is love" (4:7b–8).

God is elusive because of His boundlessness. No religion can claim to know all there is to know about God. Each religion, and each practitioner of religion, can only claim to know a part of God. But this is a startling claim that the

First Letter of John makes, that to love is to know God. I take this to mean that there is something about loving another human being that participates in the reality that is God. For those who desire to know the nature of God, indeed to "know" God, this is very significant because it plots a pathway to the Divine Mystery. It beckons to those who want to experience the divine: "If you want to know God, you will find God in the loving of another person."

It is in marriage that this love for another person, one who is not your own blood, reaches its deepest and fullest expression. It is in marriage, at least in its ideal form, that the love for another person reaches its pinnacle, in which the love, care, and regard for another equal and occasionally exceed the love of one's self.

Christians believe marriage to be a sacrament. That is, it is a place in which God promises to show up. Christian theology maintains that in loving another human being, a love that at times becomes selfless, we have a window into the kind of love God has for us, which is infinitely selfless. In those moments in which I care more deeply for the welfare, happiness, and joy of my spouse than for my own, I get a glimpse of the infinitely selfless love God has for me and all humankind. Indeed, it is the way we come to "know" God.

One of the truest things I know about marriage is that over the years, one learns so many things about one's spouse—the good, the bad, and the ugly. I know what makes him feel good about himself, what he hopes for, and who he hopes to be. I know what brings him joy and makes him lighthearted. In addition to learning what makes my spouse happy, I learn what is likely to eat away at his self-esteem, what makes him feel put down, less than worthy, and unacceptable. I know what triggers his shame, what causes him embarrassment, and what stimulates his remembrances of pain and heartache. That knowledge gives each partner in a relationship a huge amount of power over the other. That knowledge can be used to build up the other or to tear him down. And when I am angry, or when we are in the middle of a fight, I am sorely tempted to use my knowledge of him to throw a punch "below the belt" and to use my knowledge of his vulnerabilities to "win."

One of the purposes of marriage, then, is to create a mutually safe environment in which two people live out their lives in each other's presence while minimizing the potential hurt along the way. The vows of marriage, at least in theory, create a safe haven for both to grow and flourish. In theory, marriage is the safest place to be, since one is with the one other person who is most likely to long for and work for our well-being and least likely to use our vulnerabilities to hurt us.

Of course, as we know all too well, being married does not preclude hurt and violation of trust. In anger, one spouse is tempted to use against the other the very things known to be the most hurtful, for the precise reason of inflicting the most harm. But in the context of marriage, one has a commitment to be in this for the long haul. Every word spoken, every action taken, must be seen in light of its contribution toward the long-term stability of that relationship or its contribution to the relationship's demise. Such an atmosphere of mutual trust, created by the bonds and vows of marriage, offers the best opportunity for a fulfilling life together, not to mention the best environment in which to raise children.

And here is the salient point related to our conversation about gay marriage: All of this applies to couples of the same gender. Nothing in the foregoing discussion is any less true for two people of the same gender than for two people of the opposite gender. The context provided by a relationship that is mutually committed and mutually trustworthy is as important to a homosexual couple as to their heterosexual counterpart.

Sexual intimacy is a microcosm of the vulnerability shared and held in a relationship. Nakedness in the presence of another has long been a symbol for vulnerability, assisted no doubt by the fact that most of us are not entirely satisfied with the way we look. To expose to the view of someone else the body parts that are most displeasing to us is an act of vulnerability. To do so is to make ourselves open to the ridicule we already feel about ourselves and to have our worst fears confirmed. No wonder that nakedness and sexual intimacy have become symbols of all the ways in which we are vulnerable in our relationships.

When I was having my "birds and bees" talk with my daughters, I remember saying to them that while I was worried about STDs and pregnancy, what really worried me about their sexual relationships was the risk to their emotional well-being. Sexual intimacy is safe only when the relationship and one's partner are trustworthy. One-night stands are "wrong" because they are so risky to one or both of the partners. It can hardly be said that hooking up with someone at a bar constitutes having a relationship in which there is mutual trust and trustworthiness. The likelihood of getting hurt in such a situation is high. Even if nothing untoward happens, one can leave such an experience feeling lonelier and more self-alienated than if one had actually been alone. And so religious people have emphasized the importance of sexual intimacy only in the context of marriage, or in more recent years, at least a long-term, committed, and trustworthy relationship. It just makes plain sense.

Most of us know the difference between having sex and making love. Perhaps most of us have experienced both. There is no doubt that the two experiences are radically different. Having sex with someone is scratching a biological and physiological itch, made more exciting if one's partner is attractive to you and more fun if the physical sex is good. But the level of fulfillment only goes so far.

In contrast, the experience of making love is apt to be more fulfilling and joyful because of the synchronicity of saying with my body what my heart is feeling. The integration of body and spirit is what makes sex great! When I am filled with love for someone and then get to express that love through my words and actions of sexual intimacy, the combination is simply unbeatable. The experience of integration and wholeness is profound, and the sexual intimacy itself builds up and deepens the relationship. To desire another human being and to be desired by that other human being is a metaphor for God's desire to be in a relationship with us. To connect with someone on that deep level is often described by people as a spiritual experience, and so it is. To connect with an "other" in such a way as to forget the "otherness" and to experience "oneness" is a profoundly spiritual matter. It too is a metaphor for the connectedness of all the creation to the Creator.

Again, there is nothing in this discussion of sexual intimacy that is limited to heterosexual people. Nothing about vulnerability, trustworthiness, and lovemaking is any different for same-gender couples. We believe these things about relationships and sexual intimacy within relationships regardless of the gender of the genitals involved. There is simply nothing relevant about sexual orientation in the desire we feel to be one with another human being. Why, then, would we seek to withhold from gay and lesbian people our acceptance of and support for this very human and profoundly spiritual experience?

In an odd way, divorce is an extension of "loving someone else as I would want to be loved." None of us is able to be our best selves, and few of us live up to all the promises we make in marriage. For any number of reasons, marriages fail. Arguably, fault for the marriage's breakup never resides in only one spouse. The good times are a joint effort, and so are the bad. When a marriage fails, the "institution" of divorce serves the same purpose as marriage: the meaningful living-out of "loving your neighbor as yourself."

Divorce is the process whereby a couple seeks to continue to love each other even when they don't like each other. That is, "love of neighbor" means that I will treat all people as the children of God they are. Even if I have ceased to like my spouse, much less love her or him as I once did, divorce proceedings supervised by the secular court seek to force the couple to treat each other with respect and fairness through the agreed-upon and/or court-ordered settlement. Divorce arrangements attempt fairness in the dissolution of the marriage. Neither spouse is allowed to shirk certain responsibilities, especially those related to the children of the marriage. If the couple can't decide or agree on what's fair, the court will decide for them.

Divorce is another of those "rights" that gay and lesbian couples have no access to. The fight for marriage equality is not just about tax breaks, medical decision making, and inheritance rights; it's also about the protection provided by divorce. When our relationships are not recognized by the State, the State will most often not participate in the breakup of those relationships either. Gay and lesbian couples whose relationships fail do not have the protections afforded married couples who have the right to demand fairness from the court if they can't get it voluntarily from their about-to-be-former spouse.

Most people, including gay and lesbian people, don't think of the right to divorce when they think of the right to marry. But the right to seek fairness, appropriateness, and justice in the ending of a relationship is arguably as important as seeking the sanction of the State and the Church in its beginning. Just as in heterosexual relationships, the sharing of financial resources, property, and custody of children is important in gay relationships, and these issues often become a battleground when a relationship ends. Gay and lesbian couples, unlike their straight counterparts, have no recourse in the courts for redress of grievances, fairness in the allocation of property, and appropriate access and time with the couple's children. Like it or not, heterosexual married couples must meet certain guidelines administered by the court; gay couples are on their own.

In the end, marriage is the most substantive and deep example of what every religion espouses in one form or another: love your neighbor as you would want to be loved. It's a struggle to have this kind of regard for those we don't know or those we think of as enemies (even though Jesus called us to do so). We approximate such love for our friends and even have powerfully meaningful experiences of this mutual love with our best friends. But it is marriage that becomes the laboratory for learning to love one's neighbor in radically deep and mutually satisfying ways.

That kind of love is what keeps my father at my mother's side, long after she has ceased to be able to offer anything back to him in return. It is this profound love that makes him willing to use up whatever life he has left in caring for her every need, even if it shortens his own life. He doesn't feel like a victim. Rather, his love for my mother makes him want to offer his own life in service to hers. It's not a cruel price he's begrudgingly paying; rather, it is a sacrifice he's chosen to make.

To me, my parents' marriage points to God's own love and sacrifice for us. In the Christian tradition, God sacrifices God's own life in service to us and our salvation, gladly and willingly. That is why, for me, marriage is a sacred institution; even with all its patriarchal history, faults, and shortcomings, marriage is still the best place to learn about love. And if God is love, and those who love know God and participate in the reality of God, then marriage is to be honored and cherished for the astounding opportunity it gives us. Just because in reality it falls short of such noble aspirations is not an argument against marriage but rather an acknowledgment that we cannot love perfectly as God does.

I believe in marriage. I believe it is the crucible in which we come to know most deeply about love. It is in marriage that God's will for me to love all of humankind gets focused in one person. It is impossible to love humankind if I can't love one person. That opportunity to love one person and to have that love sanctioned and supported by the culture in which we live is a right denied gay and lesbian people for countless centuries. It's time to open that opportunity to all of us. Because in the end, God believes in love.

A NOTE ON THE TYPE

This book was set in Adobe Garamond. Designed for
the Adobe Corporation by Robert Slimbach, the fonts
are based on types first cut by Claude Garamond
(c. 1480–1561). Garamond was a pupil of Geoffroy Tory
and is believed to have followed the Venetian models,
although he introduced a number of important differences, and it is to him that we owe the letter we now
know as "old style." He gave to his letters a certain
elegance and feeling of movement that won their
creator an immediate reputation and the
patronage of Francis I of France.

TYPESET BY SCRIBE, PHILADELPHIA, PENNSYLVANIA
PRINTED AND BOUND BY RR DONNELLEY,
HARRISONBURG NORTH, VIRGINIA
DESIGNED BY IRIS WEINSTEIN